Differentiated Instruction
for Social Studies
Instructions and activities for the diverse classroom

Wendy Wilson
Jack Papadonis

WALCH  PUBLISHING

The classroom teacher may reproduce materials in this book for classroom use only.
The reproduction of any part for an entire school or school system is strictly prohibited.
No part of this publication may be transmitted, stored, or recorded in any form
without written permission from the publisher.

1   2   3   4   5   6   7   8   9   10

ISBN 0-8251-5911-3

Copyright © 2006

J. Weston Walch, Publisher

P.O. Box 658 • Portland, Maine 04104-0658

Printed in the United States of America

Table of Contents

Introduction to Differentiated Instruction . . . . *iv*

The Ten Themes of the Social Studies Standards . . . . *vii*

Lesson 1: A Columbian Banquet: The Great Exchange 1

Lesson 2: Creating a Children's Book on Case Law 5

Lesson 3: A Medieval Fair 9

Lesson 4: A Museum Display on the American West 13

Lesson 5: Join the WPA and Design a Mural 19

Lesson 6: A "Who Am I?" Tea Party 23

Lesson 7: History Hall of Fame 27

Lesson 8: Stop the Presses! 35

Lesson 9: Tax Cut or Public Works Investment? 38

Lesson 10: The Powers of Congress 41

Lesson 11: Worse Than Slavery 45

Lesson 12: Make Your Own Revolution 49

Lesson 13: Where Would You Place a Settlement? 54

Lesson 14: Demographic Statistics on African Nations 57

Lesson 15: Points of Longitude and Latitude 63

Lesson 16: Creating Climographs 65

Lesson 17: A Lesson in Archaeology: Build Your Baulk 69

Lesson 18: The Ellis Island Experience: A Simulation 72

Lesson 19: The Growth of the United States, 1865–1920 82

Lesson 20: What Happened Here?—A Study of Genocide 86

Introduction to Differentiated Instruction

Differentiated Instruction for Social Studies provides twenty social studies lessons that cover many of the disciplines of a typical social studies curriculum such as American history, world history, geography, and civics. Many lessons can be adapted for use with several topics, and all of the lessons encompass several social studies strands and several of the multiple intelligences. The lessons are designed to provide you with models of differentiated instruction to meet the diverse learning needs of your students.

Carol Ann Tomlinson in *The Differentiated Classroom: Responding to the Needs of All Learners* encourages educators to look at teaching and learning in a new way. Using the phrase "One size doesn't fit all," she presents a philosophy of educational beliefs:

- Students must be seen as individuals. While students are assigned grade levels by age, they differ in their readiness to learn, their interests, and their style of learning.

- These differences are significant enough to require teachers to make accommodations and differentiate by content, process, and student products. Curriculum tells us what to teach; differentiation gives us strategies to make teaching more successful.

- Students learn best when connections are made between the curriculum, student interests, and students' previous learning experiences.

- Students should be given the opportunity to work in flexible groups. Different lessons point toward grouping students in different ways: individually, heterogeneously, homogeneously, in a whole group, by student interests, and so forth.

- There should be ongoing assessment to help plan effective instruction.

To address the diverse ways that students learn and their learning styles, we can look to Howard Gardner's eight intelligences to provide a framework. Gardner's theory of multiple intelligences encourages us to scrutinize our attitudes toward learning so that each student can learn in a more relaxed environment.

Let's explore what multiple intelligences look like in the social studies classroom.

Visual/Spatial

Perceives the visual world with accuracy; can transform and visualize three dimensions in a two-dimensional space. Encourage this intelligence by using graphs and making sketches, exploring spatial visualization problems, and using mapping activities.

iv

Verbal/Linguistic

Appreciates and understands the structure, meaning, and function of language. These students can communicate effectively in both written and verbal form. Encourage this intelligence by using class to discuss ideas, making written and oral presentations, and doing research projects.

Logical/Mathematical

Ability to recognize logical or numerical patterns and observe patterns in symbolic form. Enjoys problems requiring the use of deductive or inductive reasoning and is able to follow a chain of reasoning. Encourage this intelligence by organizing and analyzing data, designing and working with spreadsheets, working on critical-thinking and estimation problems, and helping students make predictions based on the analysis of numerical data.

Musical/Rhythmic

The ability to produce and/or appreciate rhythm and music. Students may enjoy listening to music, playing an instrument, writing music or lyrics, or moving to the rhythms associated with music. Activities related to this intelligence include using songs to illustrate skills and/or concepts.

Bodily/Kinesthetic

The ability to handle one's body with skill and control, such as dancers, sports stars, and craftspeople. Students who excel in this intelligence are often hands-on learners. Activities related to this intelligence include the use of manipulatives, involvement with hands-on activities, and permitting students to participate in activities that require movement or relate physical movements to concepts.

Interpersonal

The ability to pick up on the feelings of others. Students who excel in this intelligence like to communicate, empathize, and socialize. Activities related to this intelligence include using cooperative-learning groups, brainstorming ideas, employing a creative use of grouping (including heterogeneous, homogeneous, self-directed, and so forth), and using long-range group projects.

Intrapersonal

Understanding and being in touch with one's feelings is at the center of this intelligence. Activities related to this intelligence include encouraging students to be self-reflective and explain their reasoning, using journal questions to support metacognition, and giving students quiet time to work independently.

v

Naturalist

Naturalist intelligence deals with sensing patterns in and making connections to elements in nature. These students often like to collect, classify, or read about things from nature—rocks, fossils, butterflies, feathers, shells, and the like. Activities related to this intelligence include classifying objects based upon their commonalities, searching for patterns, and using Venn diagrams to help organize data.

The Format of the Book

The twenty reproducible lessons in this book have been developed to take advantage of a number of differentiation strategies. These include:

- Student-centered activities, where the teacher acts as a guide to foster students' self-reliance as learners

- A variety of instructional materials

- Varying approaches to assessment, including nontraditional assessment and assessment by multiple means

- Flexibility in how the teacher presents the material

- Flexible grouping options, with suggestions regarding activities that work best as individual projects, for pairs, and for small groups.

- Flexible time to complete projects according to student levels and needs

- Multiple-option assignments, where students are given a choice of ways to pursue a topic and present concepts

- Multiple perspectives on ideas and events are encouraged.

- Students are encouraged to problem-solve independently, to use their background knowledge, and to use their individual talents and skills

- Students are encouraged to make interest-based learning choices.

- Multiple intelligences are addressed in each activity, and are listed on the teacher page.

You can either use these lessons as they are presented, or adapt them to your own curriculum. The curriculum standards produced by the National Council for the Social Studies have been a guide in setting up lessons that conform to the social studies standards. It is hoped that these lessons will further serve as a springboard for you to use your own ingenuity to rework lessons to meet the unique abilities of all students.

Differentiated Instruction for Social Studies

The Ten Themes of the Social Studies Standards

In 1994, the National Council for the Social Studies approved a set of standards for the teaching of social studies nationwide. An integral part of this was the setting out of ten themes, or strands, that can serve as the organizing principle for classroom curriculum. Not only are these strands interrelated, but they are drawn from all of the social studies disciplines and social sciences so that they are broad and all-encompassing. The ten strands are

I. CULTURE

Social studies programs should include experiences that provide for the study of culture and cultural diversity.

II. TIME, CONTINUITY, AND CHANGE

Social studies programs should include experiences that provide for the study of the ways human beings view themselves in and over time.

III. PEOPLE, PLACES, AND ENVIRONMENTS

Social studies programs should include experiences that provide for the study of people, places, and environments.

IV. INDIVIDUAL DEVELOPMENT AND IDENTITY

Social studies programs should include experiences that provide for the study of individual development and identity.

V. INDIVIDUALS, GROUPS, AND INSTITUTIONS

Social studies programs should include experiences that provide for the study of interactions among individuals, groups, and institutions.

VI. POWER, AUTHORITY, AND GOVERNANCE

Social studies programs should include experiences that provide for the study of how people create and change structures of power, authority, and governance.

VII. PRODUCTION, DISTRIBUTION, AND CONSUMPTION

Social studies programs should include experiences that provide for the study of how people organize for the production, distribution, and consumption of goods and services.

VIII. SCIENCE, TECHNOLOGY, AND SOCIETY

Social studies programs should include experiences that provide for the study of relationships among science, technology, and society.

IX. GLOBAL CONNECTIONS

Social studies programs should include experiences that provide for the study of global connections and interdependence.

X. CIVIC IDEALS AND PRACTICES

Social studies programs should include experiences that provide for the study of the ideals, principles, and practices of citizenship in a democratic republic.

(From *Expectations of Excellence: Curriculum Standards for Social Studies.* Developed by the National Council for the Social Studies. Washington, D.C., 1994.)

Because of the broad nature of these strands, lessons presented in this book may reflect several strands. At the beginning of each lesson, the suggested strands will be listed by number as stated on page *vii* and above.

Differentiated Instruction for Social Studies

A Columbian Banquet: The Great Exchange

OVERVIEW

With the "discovery" of the Americas by Christopher Columbus, there was an exchange of culture and foodstuffs between the Eastern and Western hemispheres. This caused dramatic changes in the diet of Europeans and Africans, and caused substantial ecological changes in the Americas. The purpose of this lesson is to promote an understanding of the incredible impact the Columbian Exchange had on both the Old World and the New World.

SOCIAL STUDIES STRANDS

I. Culture; III. People, Places, and Environments; V. Individuals, Groups, and Institutions; VII. Production, Distribution, and Consumption; IX. Global Connections

DIFFERENTIATION STRATEGIES

- This is a student-centered activity. The teacher is a guide to facilitate students' self-reliance as learners.

- Multiple intelligences addressed: Verbal/Linguistic, Visual/Spatial, Bodily/Kinesthetic, Interpersonal, Naturalist

- Multiple-option assignments are used. Students have a choice of ways to pursue the concepts in this lesson.

- A variety of materials can be used to facilitate student learning.

- Time can be used flexibly in accordance with student levels and needs. This lesson provides flexibility in how much time the teacher wishes to allot to the activities.

- This lesson provides flexible grouping, lending itself to either individual or group work.

- Students are assessed in multiple ways.

WHAT TO DO

There are a number of ways to teach this lesson. A suggestion for a simple lesson appears on page 2, showing the steps you would follow.

1

1. Have students draw slips of paper on each of which is written the name of a foodstuff. It could be a spice, a vegetable, a fruit, a flower, or a grain, or it might be an animal.

2. Have students research the foodstuff. They should prepare to tell the class whether it originated in the Old World or New World, and what impact this product had as it moved from one world to the other.

3. If time and circumstances permit, students could draw a picture of this product or bring in a sample for the class to share. A "banquet" could be set up where the class can sample the food products. As an example—for corn or maize, a student could bake corn bread for the class.

Be certain to tell the class not to bring in peanuts or nuts, as there may be students sensitive to these products in particular. You can tell students that peanuts, cashews, and pecans are New World in origin and that peanuts in particular became an important cash crop in Africa.

VARIATIONS

• Students (either individually or in groups) could draw a map showing the two hemispheres and the originating area of the foodstuff.

• Students could compile a "Columbian" recipe book using the food products that the exchange brings to Europe.

• Students could research a typical meal of a European before the exchange and after the exchange.

• Students could research the ecological changes wrought by the exchange. (For example, pigs brought by the Spanish to the New World destroyed entire areas of foliage.)

ASSESSMENT

You can assess students on their oral presentation, their written work, their attention to the task, or their class discussion work.

Answers

NEW WORLD			OLD WORLD	
avocadoes	peaches	tobacco	apples	oats
black-eyed Susans	peanuts	tomatoes	bananas	onions
blueberries	pears	vanilla	barley	okra
cashews	pecans	yams	cattle	pigs
cassava root (manioc,	peppers	zucchini	chicken	olives
tapioca)	petunias		crabgrass	rice
chocolate	pineapple		citrus fruit	sheep
corn	pole beans		daffodils	soybeans
dahlias	potatoes		daisies	sugar cane
gum	pumpkins		dandelions	tulips
kidney beans	quinine		honeybees	watermelon
lima beans	rubber		horses	wheat
marigolds	squash		lettuce	wine grapes
navy beans	sunflowers		lilacs	

Differentiated Instruction for Social Studies

A Columbian Banquet: The Great Exchange

Cut into individual slips.

corn	cassava root (manioc or tapioca)	chocolate
watermelon	crabgrass	sheep
potatoes	avocadoes	vanilla
peaches	tulips	chickens
tomatoes	pineapple	petunias
pears	daisies	honeybees
peppers	yams	black-eyed Susans
apples	daffodils	rice
lima beans	zucchini	wheat
citrus fruit	lilacs	barley
kidney beans	blueberries	oats
bananas	horses	sugarcane
pumpkin	sunflowers	onions
olives	cattle	lettuce
squash	gum	okra
dandelions	pigs	dahlias

A Columbian Banquet: The Great Exchange

One of the most dramatic events in history was the exchange of foodstuffs and other products between the Old World and the New World after the voyages of Christopher Columbus to the Americas and the subsequent European expansion into the Western Hemisphere. We will explore this exchange by investigating the foodstuffs that were exchanged and how they affected people's lives on both sides of the Atlantic Ocean.

DIRECTIONS

In class, you will draw a slip of paper out of a hat or bag. On that slip is the name of a foodstuff or other natural product—it could be a spice, a vegetable, a fruit, a flower, a grain, or an animal. Your task is to research this product and be prepared to tell the class whether it originated in the Old World or New World. What was the impact of this plant's or animal's exchange from one world to the other? You might wish to draw a picture of this product. You might even bring in a sample for the class to try. Check with your teacher first to make sure that is appropriate and that no one is allergic to it.

Name: _____

Foodstuff/animal/plant selected:_____

Old World or New World Origin?_____

Uses:

Impact on area brought into:

Picture or drawing of item:

Creating a Children's Book on Case Law

OVERVIEW

This lesson looks at some of the key Supreme Court decisions that have affected our lives over the past fifty years. The cases have been chosen not only for their importance in American history but also for their scope and variety.

SOCIAL STUDIES STRANDS

I. Culture; V. Individuals, Groups, and Institutions; VI. Power, Authority, and Governance; X. Civic Ideals and Practices

DIFFERENTIATION STRATEGIES

- Multiple intelligences addessed: Verbal/Linguistic, Visual/Spatial, Logical/Mathematical, Interpersonal, Intrapersonal

- This is a student-centered activity. The teacher is a guide to facilitate students' self-reliance as learners.

- This activity provides flexible grouping: This lesson can be done individually, in pairs, or in triads.

- Time can be used flexibly in configuring this lesson to meet students' learning levels and needs.

- Students use their essential skills to understand key concepts and principles.

- Multiple-option assignments are used. Students have flexibility in how they can present the concepts in this lesson.

- Multiple perspectives on ideas and events are promoted: Students have flexibility and latitude in presenting their ideas.

- Students are assessed in multiple ways.

WHAT TO DO

Following the directions on the student activity pages, students create a children's book on a Supreme Court case. This is a good exercise for group discussion as well as personal reflection. It uses the students' analytical and computer research skills, and it can employ their artistic talents. It might be fun for students to "try out" their final product on younger siblings or younger students to see if their explanations of the Supreme Court case are really clear and understandable.

A grading rubric is included. You can assign the rubric's point values to the categories or use the rubric to customize your own point system.

ASSESSMENT

This lesson provides nontraditional methods of assessment. An optional scoring rubric follows.

Name:_____   Teacher: _____

Date: _____   Title of Work: _____

	Criteria				Points
Content Knowledge	The book does not demonstrate complete grasp of the information.	The book demonstrates basic content information.	The book demonstrates full concept and information but does not elaborate.	The book demonstrates full concept and content information and elaborates.	_____
Historical Accuracy	There are five or more errors in historical accuracy.	There are three or four errors in historical accuracy.	There are one or two errors in historical accuracy.	There are no errors in historical accuracy.	_____
Position Paragraph	Statement of position cannot be determined. Evidence is unrelated to argument.	Position is stated, but is not maintained consistently throughout work. Argument is supported by limited evidence.	Position is clearly stated and consistently maintained. References to the issue(s) at hand are missing. Evidence clearly supports the position.	Position is clearly stated and consistently maintained. Clear references to the issue(s) are stated. Evidence clearly supports the position.	_____
Graphics/ Pictures	Graphics do not go with the accompanying text or appear to be randomly chosen.	Graphics go well with the text, but there are too few and the book seems "text-heavy."	Graphics go well with the text, but there are so many that they distract from the text.	Graphics go well with the text, and there is a good mix of text and graphics.	_____
Attractiveness and Organization	The book's formatting and organization of material are confusing to the reader.	The book has well-organized information.	The book has attractive formatting and well-organized information.	The book has exceptionally attractive formatting and well-organized information.	_____
Language Mechanics	There are five or more errors in writing mechanics and spelling.	There are three or four errors in writing mechanics and spelling.	There are one or two errors in writing mechanics and spelling.	There are no errors in writing mechanics and spelling.	_____
Sources	Most sources are not accurately documented.	All sources (information and graphics) are accurately documented, but many are not in the desired format.	All sources (information and graphics) are accurately documented, but a few are not in the desired format.	All sources (information and graphics) are accurately documented in the desired format.	_____
				Total →	_____

Creating a Children's Book on Case Law

Directions: Individually or in partnership pairs or triads, you are to choose a Supreme Court case from the list on page 8, research the case, and create a children's picture book regarding the case. The book should contain both text and pictures and should be at least fifteen pages long. Additionally, each student should prepare a three-paragraph essay detailing her or his opinion of the Supreme Court's decision.

Focusing Your Research

Use the five W's to help focus your research:

Who is involved in the case? Who would be good people to quote in your presentation? Who wrote the majority opinion? Who wrote the dissenting opinion, if there was one? Who wrote concurring opinions?

What are the issues of the opposing sides of the case? These are the "facts of the case."

When was this case argued before the Supreme Court? When was a decision rendered? When did the issue first arise or how long has it been debated?

Where in the Constitution will you find the basis for the Court's decision? Which Article or Amendment?

Why is the issue being debated or challenged?

Organizing Your Children's Book

Here is a suggested outline for you to follow.

I. Introduction

   A. Who was involved?

   B. When did it happen?

   C. What is the connection to the Constitution?

II. Facts of the case

(continued)

Creating a Children's Book on Case Law *(continued)*

III. Supreme Court decision

    A. Summarize the majority opinion (and concurring opinions, if any).

    B. Summarize the dissenting opinions, if any.

IV. Effects of the decision on U.S. history

Each group will be assessed on the quality of the children's book it crafts. No, your skills as an artist will NOT be the sole basis of the evaluation.

Essay

Each person will write a persuasive three-paragraph essay expressing his/her individual opinion on the Supreme Court's decision. Do you agree or disagree with the decision?

Part of your grade will include your research during class time in the library and partnership evaluation.

CONSTITUTIONAL LAW CASES

1. *Plessy* v. *Ferguson* (1896)
2. *Brown* v. *Board of Education of Topeka* (1954)
3. *Gideon* v. *Wainwright* (1963)
4. *Heart of Atlanta Motel* v. *United States* (1964)
5. *Miranda* v. *Arizona* (1966)
6. *Tinker* v. *Des Moines School District* (1969)
7. *Roe* v. *Wade* (1973)
8. *United States* v. *Nixon* (1974)
9. *Goss* v. *Lopez* (1975)
10. *University of California* v. *Bakke* (1978)
11. *New Jersey* v. *T.L.O.* (1984)
12. *Hazelwood* v. *Kuhlmeier* (1988)
13. *Texas* v. *Johnson* (1989)
14. *Harris* v. *Forklift Systems, Inc.* (1993)
15. *United States* v. *Lopez* (1994)
16. *Hurley* v. *Irish-American Gay Group of Boston* (1995)
17. *Veronia School District* v. *Acton* (1995)
18. *United States* v. *Virginia* (1996)
19. *Reno* v. *ACLU* (1997)
20. *Boy Scouts of America* v. *Dale* (2000)
21. *Bush* v. *Gore* (2000)
22. *PGA Tour, Inc.* v. *Martin* (2001)

A Medieval Fair

OVERVIEW

In the early part of the Middle Ages (c. 500–1100), manors and towns existed pretty much in isolation from one another. After c.1100, there was an increase in trade, commerce, and travel. Many medieval villages and towns held fairs where traveling merchants and local craftspeople could demonstrate and sell their wares. Traveling troupes of players would perform dramatic pieces, songs, or poems to entertain the crowds. This lesson gives students a chance to re-create a medieval fair and engage in some activities that can tap into their unique interests and talents.

SOCIAL STUDIES STRANDS

I. Culture; III. People, Places, and Environments; IV. Individual Development and Identity; V. Individuals, Groups, and Institutions; VI. Power, Authority, and Governance; VII. Production, Distribution, and Consumption; VIII. Science, Technology, and Society

DIFFERENTIATION STRATEGIES

- This is a student-centered activity. The teacher is a guide to facilitate students' self-reliance as learners.

- Multiple intelligences addressed: Verbal/Linguistic, Logical/Mathematical, Visual/Spatial, Bodily/Kinesthetic, Musical/Rhythmic, Interpersonal, Intrapersonal, Naturalist

- This lesson provides flexible grouping. It can be done individually, in pairs, or in groups.

- Time can be used flexibly in configuring this lesson to meet students' learning levels and needs. Teachers can be extremely flexible in the time that they allot to this project. It can be done in or out of class.

- Multiple-option assignments are used. Students are presented with a variety of topics that they can pursue according to their skills and interests.

- Teachers are encouraged to guide students into making interest-based choices for their project.

- Students are assessed in multiple ways.

WHAT TO DO

This lesson is highly appropriate for use as a culminating lesson after a study of the Middle Ages in world history. A variety of projects are available, described on the accompanying student pages. Students must use research skills to investigate their particular activity, then design their project and carry out its implementation.

ASSESSMENT

This lesson provides nontraditional methods of assessment. For example, an excellent method of assessment for this project would be to have another class of students (perhaps from another grade level) visit the fair to make comments and ask questions on the various projects, much as is done at a science fair.

A Medieval Fair

After about 1100 C.E., when transportation and communication improved in western Europe, traveling merchants and performers went from town to town selling their wares or displaying their talents. Local craftspeople and farmers also sold their products to the general public. People in both the town and the surrounding rural area greatly looked forward to these fairs, which were often held to correspond with a festival of the church.

Directions: Individually or in groups or pairs, choose and create an activity or product that might be presented at a medieval fair. Try to be as authentic as possible with your design or performance. No doubt you will have to do some research to find out about your particular craft or product.

Possible options to present at the fair

- Build a model of a working catapult.

- Make a stained-glass window from transparent colored paper.

- Design the first page of an illuminated manuscript.

- Make a demonstration on how to dye fabric using products from nature (for example, onion skins or goldenrod).

- Write and perform a chivalric epic poem.

- Weave a basket.

- Stitch a needlepoint.

- Create a coat of arms for your family.

- Prepare a display of spices that might be purchased from a traveling merchant, and list their uses.

- Make an illustrated medieval recipe book.

- Write and/or perform a medieval miracle or mystery play.

- Build a model of a castle or cathedral.

- Draw a poster to attract people to the fair. (Remember that most people were illiterate during medieval times.)

(continued)

A Medieval Fair (continued)

Name_____ Date _____

Project I have chosen to present at the fair:

_____

_____

_____

Materials I will use/need:_____

_____

_____

Potential audience or customers for my talents at the fair: _____

_____

_____

_____

_____

How does this project relate to life in the Middle Ages?

_____

_____

_____

_____

_____

_____

_____

Differentiated Instruction for Social Studies

A Museum Display on the American West

OVERVIEW

This lesson is designed to be a culminating activity in the study of the westward expansion of the United States. Students will have to decide what they want museumgoers to know about the American West and how they can best get this knowledge across in an interesting, visual way.

SOCIAL STUDIES STRANDS

I. Culture; II. Time, Continuity, and Change; III. People, Places, and Environments; V. Individuals, Groups, and Institutions; VII. Production, Distribution, and Consumption; VIII. Science, Technology, and Society; IX. Global Connections; X. Civic Ideals and Practices

DIFFERENTIATION STRATEGIES

- This is a student-centered activity. The teacher is a guide to facilitate students' self-reliance as learners.

- Multiple intelligences addressed: Verbal/Linguistic, Logical/Mathematical, Visual/Spatial, Musical/Rhythmic, Interpersonal, Intrapersonal, Naturalist

- This lesson provides flexible grouping. It lends itself to either individual or group work.

- Multiple-option assignments are used. Students are given options on ways to pursue the concepts in this lesson.

- Time can be used flexibly in accordance with student levels and needs.

- Students can be guided to make interest-based learning choices using their own unique skills and talents.

- Multiple types of materials are provided.

- Students are assessed in multiple ways.

WHAT TO DO

1. Ask students to think about museums that they have visited and exhibits that held their interest. Did the exhibits include photographs, paintings, artifacts, a video or an audio recording, a model or an exact replica? More and more museums are using audio presentations, such as music and video recordings, to supplement their collections and give a background flavor to the time period or topic being shown. The American West has a rich musical heritage.

2. This lesson can be done on many levels. It can be designed as it is set out here, or students can take an extra step and make the display cards for their exhibits. If your school has space, you could even set up a museum room designed by your students in which they have reproduced the artifacts and visual images they have selected.

ASSESSMENT

In assessing this lesson, the important concern is not the quality of the objects students reproduce but the thought process behind the choices students have made.

Differentiated Instruction for Social Studies

A Museum Display on the American West

You have been hired to design a room in a new museum of American history. The title of this room is "The American West—Yesterday and Today." The room is 25 feet by 25 feet with a center room divider that is 10 feet long. Display cases line the walls. You may also use freestanding displays on the floor space. Remember, though, to leave space for people to move through the exhibit area. A floor plan of your room is provided below. The wall displays should cover these topics: The West 1820–1840, The West 1840–1860, The West 1860–1890, and The West in Popular Culture Today. You may choose the subject for the display on the center room divider.

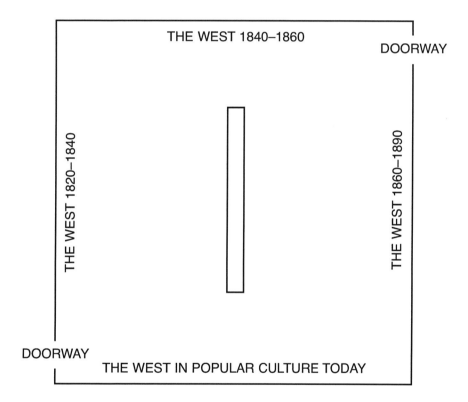

What will you display on each wall? What photographs will you use? (Remember that photography really was not used until the 1850s.) What paintings will you display? what maps? diagrams? You should also display artifacts—human-made objects from the specific time period. In the spaces provided on the next three pages, list your choices. You should think about what would make your displays visually appealing and of interest to your audience, the museumgoer. The displays must also be historically accurate!

(continued)

Differentiated Instruction for Social Studies

A Museum Display on the American West *(continued)*

THE WEST 1820–1840	THE WEST 1840–1860
photos/paintings	photos/paintings
maps/diagrams	maps/diagrams
artifacts	artifacts
other ideas?	other ideas?

(continued)

Lesson 4

Differentiated Instruction for Social Studies

A Museum Display on the American West *(continued)*

THE WEST 1860–1890

photos/paintings

_____

_____

_____

_____

maps/diagrams

_____

_____

_____

artifacts

_____

_____

_____

_____

other ideas?

_____

_____

_____

_____

THE WEST IN POPULAR CULTURE TODAY

photos/paintings

_____

_____

_____

_____

maps/diagrams

_____

_____

_____

artifacts

_____

_____

_____

_____

other ideas?

_____

_____

_____

_____

(continued)

A Museum Display on the American West *(continued)*

CENTER DIVIDER

Topic: _____

photos/paintings

_____

_____

_____

_____

maps/diagrams

_____

_____

_____

artifacts

_____

_____

_____

other ideas?

_____

_____

FREESTANDING DISPLAYS

_____

_____

_____

_____

artifacts

_____

_____

_____

other ideas?

_____

_____

EXTRA CHALLENGE

Using 3" × 5" or 4" × 6" cards, write museum display information for the items you have chosen. You should give the title of the photo, painting, map, diagram, or artifact, who produced it, and the date. Write a paragraph explaining each item's significance in the history of the West during this time period.

Sample: **Oil Painting:** *The Oregon Trail* (1869) by Albert Bierstadt. Bierstadt was born in Dusseldorf, Germany, but was brought up in Massachusetts. He painted this wagon train after traveling west over the Oregon Trail. Note the oxen pulling the wagon and the emigrants driving their herds of farm animals. The entire scene is bathed in the light of the setting sun as if the golden future was in the West. Paintings such as this romanticized the journey to the West.

Differentiated Instruction for Social Studies

Join the WPA and Design a Mural

OVERVIEW

One of the key features of President Franklin Roosevelt's New Deal was the WPA, the Works Progress Administration. The WPA was a massive public works project that put people to work not just on traditional projects such as building dams and bridges, but also on such projects as public buildings (including interior decoration, which might be a mural or sculpture), oral and written history projects, and a federally funded theater project.

These projects were designed not just to give people jobs but also to celebrate the United States and instill in the public a sense of history and pride. Sometimes this brought the artists into direct conflict with the government administrators, such as when Orson Welles and John Houseman tried to produce a play called *The Cradle Will Rock.* The play was critical of the American economic and social system. Similarly, the artists who painted an enormous mural inside the Coit Tower in San Francisco presented scenes of typical American life—farmers plowing their fields and harvesting, city life, transportation, and people reading in a public library. On closer inspection, though, you can see a man reaching for *Das Kapital,* Karl Marx's most famous work on communism. The McCarthy era was in the 1950s; the New Deal was in the 1930s.

SOCIAL STUDIES STRANDS

I. Culture; II. Time, Continuity, and Change; III. People, Places, and Environments; IV. Individual Development and Identity; V. Individuals, Groups, and Institutions; VI. Power, Authority, and Governance; VII. Production, Distribution, and Consumption; VIII. Science, Technology, and Society; X. Civic Ideals and Practices

DIFFERENTIATION STRATEGIES

- This is a student-centered activity. The teacher is a guide to facilitate students' self-reliance as learners.

- Multiple intelligences addressed: Visual/Spatial, Interpersonal, Intrapersonal, Naturalist

- Multiple-option assignments are used. Students are given options on ways to pursue the concepts in this lesson.

- This lesson provides flexible grouping. It lends itself very well to group work.

- Time can be used flexibly in accordance with student levels and needs.

- Students can be guided to make interest-based learning choices.

- Students are encouraged to problem-solve, and multiple perspectives on ideas and events are acknowledged.

- Multiple types of materials are provided.

- This lesson provides an opportunity for students to use their skills and knowledge of the subject area to make reflective choices in how they present their project.

- Students are assessed in multiple ways.

WHAT TO DO

In this lesson, have students design and possibly even construct a mural showing American life during the 1930s. This lends itself well to group work. There are many web sites that show the Coit Tower murals and other WPA projects, so students can do research before designing their murals or can simply compare their final project with an actual WPA work.

VARIATIONS

This lesson could also be adapted to another period in American history. The key is to have students reflect on life in the United States at that time period.

ASSESSMENT

The discussion and preplanning are more important than the actual product, since students really need to reflect on American values, economy, and way of life.

Join the WPA and Design a Mural

Directions: The year is 1934, and—lucky you! You have been hired by the Works Progress Administration to decorate a new courthouse in Albany, New York. Your project is to design a mural celebrating American life. What will you choose for your images? What occupations will you show? What cultural institutions? city life or country life, or both? Will you show people standing in breadlines? idle factories? Or will you gloss over the Great Depression and try to show a revitalized America? You are required to include these things in your mural:

- cityscape (for the city of your choice)

- people at work

- people at play

- cultural events/institutions

- educational institutions

- national landmarks (at least three)

- representations of at least four geographical regions of North America, including their natural resources

- governmental institutions

- most common types of transportation and communication

- anything else you feel is representative of the American people and way of life during that time period

(continued)

Join the WPA and Design a Mural *(continued)*

A list of what my/our mural will picture

Cityscape I /we will show: _____

_____

How I/we will show people at work: _____

_____

How I/we will show people at play: _____

_____

Cultural events/institutions I/we will show: _____

_____

Educational institutions I/we will show: _____

_____

National landmarks (at least three) I/we will show: _____

_____

Representations of at least four geographical regions of North America,
including their natural resources: _____

_____

Governmental institutions I/we will show: _____

_____

Most common types of transportation and communication: _____

_____

Other things I/we will show on my/our mural: _____

_____

Lesson 5

Differentiated Instruction for Social Studies

A "Who Am I?" Tea Party

OVERVIEW

This lesson is a great review vehicle for any history course. It can be adapted for American history, world history, or European history, and deals with people who have made their mark on a particular time period through their political, social, cultural, or scientific/technological contributions. The lesson as it is presented here is appropriate for a world civilizations class such as one encompassing the ancient world, classical civilizations, and the Middle Ages.

SOCIAL STUDIES STRANDS

I. Culture; II. Time, Continuity, and Change; III. People, Places, and Environments; IV. Individual Development and Identity; V. Individuals, Groups, and Institutions; VI. Power, Authority and Governance; VIII. Science, Technology, and Society; IX. Global Connections

DIFFERENTIATION STRATEGIES

- This is a student-centered activity. The teacher is a guide to facilitate students' self-reliance as learners.

- Multiple intelligences addressed: Verbal/Linguistic, Visual/Spatial, Bodily/Kinesthetic, Musical, Interpersonal, Intrapersonal

- Multiple-option assignments are used. Students are given a variety of ways to pursue the concepts in this lesson.

- Time can be used flexibly in accordance with student levels and needs.

- Students can be guided to make interest-based learning choices.

- This lesson provides an opportunity for students to use their skills and knowledge of the subject area to make reflective choices in how they present their project.

- This project allows the teacher flexibility in how the project is presented.

- Students can be assessed in multiple ways.

WHAT TO DO

1. Make a copy of the list of names provided, and cut the names into separate slips. Each student should draw a name. Students should not tell their classmates which name they have picked.

2. Students should then research their historical figure, concentrating on why he or she is significant for this time period. Is he or she a political leader? a writer? an inventor or scientist? How did this person's contributions affect the age in which he or she lived?

3. Once students have finished their research, provide each student with a complete list of names. Have students ask each other questions to try to identify the name each classmate chose. You might encourage students to provide hints. For example, they could dress in period costume, or carry something representative of their assigned person (a copy of a painting, a quote from one of their works, a model of an invention). As students identify the person who drew each name, they should check off the name on the list.

4. The student who finds all the people first and completes the list wins. However, the real point of the exercise is not to win, but to mix and discuss.

ASSESSMENT

This lesson can be a springboard for a discussion of change and whether it is a time period that can cause great people to rise to the fore or whether it is just fate that causes such innovators to appear.

Differentiated Instruction for Social Studies

FAMOUS PEOPLE OF EARLY HISTORY

Cut this list into individual slips, and have students draw the slips of paper to be assigned their historical figure.

Alexander the Great	Hammurabi	Octavian Augustus
Archimedes	Hatshepsut	Plato
Catherine of Siena	Hildegard of Bingen	Pythagoras
Chandragupta	Hippocrates	Sargon of Akkad
Charlemagne	Joan of Arc	Sophocles
Ch'in Shih Huang Ti	Justinian	Spartacus
Confucius	Leif Eriksson	Thomas Aquinas
Eleanor of Aquitaine	Mansa Musa	Thucydides
Gautama Siddhartha (Buddha)	Marco Polo	Tutankhamen
Geoffrey Chaucer	Murasaki Shikibu	Zheng He

Differentiated Instruction for Social Studies   © 2006 Walch Publishing

A "Who Am I?" Tea Party

At various times in history, certain individuals have made their mark on their time period and on history in general.

You are going to become one of these important figures. You will be asked to draw a name taken from the list below. Do not tell your classmates who you have drawn. Research this person's life and, most importantly, his or her contribution to the time period. How did this contribution change society, culture, politics, or economics of the time?

Once your research is complete, you will join your classmates at a "Who Am I?" party. Try to guess who your classmates are by asking judicious questions, while they do the same to you. As you "discover" a person, check off the name on the list.

_____ Alexander the Great   _____ Justinian

_____ Archimedes   _____ Leif Eriksson

_____ Catherine of Siena   _____ Mansa Musa

_____ Chandragupta   _____ Marco Polo

_____ Charlemagne   _____ Murasaki Shikibu

_____ Ch'in Shih Huang Ti   _____ Octavian Augustus

_____ Confucius   _____ Plato

_____ Eleanor of Aquitaine   _____ Pythagoras

_____ Gautama Siddhartha (Buddha)   _____ Sargon of Akkad

_____ Geoffrey Chaucer   _____ Sophocles

_____ Hammurabi   _____ Spartacus

_____ Hatshepsut   _____ Thomas Aquinas

_____ Hildegard of Bingen   _____ Thucydides

_____ Hippocrates   _____ Tutankhamen

_____ Joan of Arc   _____ Zheng He

Lesson 6

Differentiated Instruction for Social Studies

History Hall of Fame

OVERVIEW

This lesson helps students understand what determines the importance of historical events and how things that have happened in history can affect a region or have worldwide significance. In this lesson, students see events from the perspective of various social scientists and gain an understanding of the interconnectivity of political, social, cultural, and economic consequences.

SOCIAL STUDIES STRANDS

I. Culture; II. Time, Continuity, and Change; III. People, Places, and Environments; IV. Individual Development and Identity; V. Individuals, Groups, and Institutions; VI. Power, Authority, and Governance; VII. Production, Distribution, and Consumption; VIII. Science, Technology, and Society; IX. Global Connections; X. Civic Ideals and Practices

DIFFERENTIATION STRATEGIES

- This is a student-centered activity. The teacher is a guide to facilitate students' self-reliance as learners.

- Multiple intelligences addressed: Verbal/Linguistic, Logical/Mathematical, Interpersonal, Intrapersonal, Visual/Spatial, Naturalist

- Multiple-option assignments are used. Students are given options on ways to pursue the concepts in this lesson.

- This lesson provides flexible grouping. It lends itself well to group work.

- Time can be used flexibly in accordance with student levels and needs.

- Students can be guided to make interest-based learning choices.

- Students are encouraged to problem-solve, and multiple perspectives on ideas and events are acknowledged.

- The method of assessment is clear and known to students ahead of time.

- Students are asked to use their essential skills and knowledge of the subject matter to make reflective choices in their presentations.

WHAT TO DO

1. Assign students to six research teams (one for each event) for which each student will assume the role of a historian, a sociologist, an economist, or a political scientist in evaluating events for selection into the History Hall of Fame.

2. Have students perform research on the events listed. This lesson lends itself well to web-based research.

3. Two lessons are presented. One is based on U.S. history and one can be used for a world history class. Feel free to add your own events. For U.S. history, you might add the assassination of President Kennedy. For world history, you could add the Yom Kippur War, the Hungarian uprising, or the Chernobyl nuclear disaster.

ASSESSMENT

The resulting presentations should be multimedia rather than traditional debates or essays. A grading rubric is provided for assessment. It is addressed to the student so that it can be passed out to groups ahead of time to communicate exactly how they will be evaluated.

EVALUATION RUBRIC FOR THE HISTORY HALL OF FAME PROJECT

As you research your event and work with your group on the presentation, keep in mind the descriptors listed below in the rubric. This will be a combination of individual and group assessment.

	Poor 5 points	Fair 10 points	Satisfactory 15 points	Superior 20 points
Historical content and concepts	The project demonstrates some, but not complete, basic content information.	The project demonstrates basic content information but incomplete concept connections.	The project demonstrates content and concept information but does not elaborate.	The exhibit demonstrates full content and concept information and elaborates.
Historical accuracy	There are three or more errors in historical accuracy.	There are two errors in historical accuracy.	There is one error in historical accuracy.	There are no errors in historical accuracy.
Meeting project requirements	The project is missing three or more required elements.	The project is missing two required elements.	The project is missing one required element.	All required elements are present.
Multimedia presentation's organization and effectiveness	The presentation's formatting, attention to detail, and language mechanics are confusing.	The presentation's formatting, attention to detail, and language mechanics are acceptable.	The presentation has an attractive format and is well organized.	The presentation has an exceptionally attractive format, is well organized, and contains no errors in language mechanics.
Student productivity	Student does not work productively and effectively during research and preparation time.	Student works productively and effectively during some research and preparation time.	Student works productively and effectively during most research and preparation time.	Student works productively and effectively during all research and preparation time.

Welcome to the U.S. History Hall of Fame

What determines the importance of historical events? Your team of researchers has just been appointed by the board of directors of the American History Hall of Fame to evaluate one of the following six events from the last half of the twentieth century for induction into the History Hall of Fame:

1. Montgomery Bus Boycott

2. invention of the personal computer

3. 1968 Democratic National Convention

4. first lunar landing

5. Watergate scandal

6. legalization of the birth control pill

Only one of these events will be selected as this year's inductee.

THE TASK

To arrive at an in-depth understanding of these historical events, we will divide the class into six groups. Each group will research, analyze, organize, and then present to the Hall of Fame's board of directors an evaluation of its assigned event. This presentation will be in a multimedia format (for example, a Power Point presentation, an iMovie, or a video clip).

Each group's evaluation will be structured to address the following categories:

- historical context
- economic consequences
- social significance
- political implications

By the end of this project, you will be familiar with the key individuals and groups that shaped these events during the last half of the twentieth century.

THE PROCESS

Your research and analysis should focus on the four main categories listed in the task section above. Each group's presentation should give the board of directors a logical evaluation of the event's importance in U.S. history.

(continued)

Welcome to the U.S. History Hall of Fame *(continued)*

To accomplish your task, these steps must be followed:

1. First, you will be assigned to a research team.

2. Each team member will assume a role to aid in the investigation: historian, sociologist, economist, or political scientist.

3. Each team will spend six class sessions using web sites to research the event and two class sessions planning a seven-minute multimedia presentation. Final production will be done using out-of-class time.

4. Each group must turn in a bibliography of resources on the day of their presentation.

Each project must include the following four elements:

- seven-minute multimedia presentation

- annotated bibliography of all web sites

- 500-word typed paper that describes how the research was conducted and how the presentation was created and developed

- time line (from 1950–2000) of fifteen historical events associated with the nominated event

RESEARCH PARAMETERS

Each role has essential elements that must be addressed in the presentation:

Historian

1. Who were the key individuals involved in the event?

2. What were the principal causes of the event?

3. How has this event influenced history since it occurred?

(continued)

Lesson 7

Differentiated Instruction for Social Studies

Welcome to the U.S. History Hall of Fame *(continued)*

Sociologist

1. What was society like before the event?

2. How has society changed as a result of this event?

3. What was the importance of technology in the event's development?

Economist

1. Who were the leading economic figures associated with the event?

2. What did it cost, and how was it funded?

3. What was the event's long-lasting economic impact?

Political Scientist

1. Who were the key politicians of the time?

2. What role did political parties play during the event?

3. What was the relationship between the event and the Constitution or the nation's laws?

CONCLUSION

After completing this project, you should be able to make a strong case to say why the event you researched is worthy of being enshrined in the U.S. History Hall of Fame.

Welcome to the World History Hall of Fame

What determines the importance of historical events? Your team of researchers has just been appointed by the board of directors of the World History Hall of Fame to evaluate one of the following six events from the last half of the twentieth century for induction into the World History Hall of Fame:

1. the launching of *Sputnik*

2. the invention of the personal computer

3. the formation of the European Economic Community

4. the fall of the Berlin Wall

5. the end of apartheid

6. Tiananmen Square

Only one of these events will be selected as this year's inductee.

THE TASK

To arrive at an in-depth understanding of these historical events, we will divide the class into six groups. Each group will research, analyze, organize, and then present to the Hall of Fame's board of directors an evaluation of its assigned event. This presentation will be in a multimedia format (for example, a Power Point presentation, an iMovie, or a video clip).

Each group's evaluation will be structured to address the following categories:

- historical context
- economic consequences
- social significance
- political implications

By the end of this project, you will be familiar with the key individuals and groups that shaped these events during the last half of the twentieth century.

THE PROCESS

Your research and analysis should focus on the four main categories listed in the task section above. Each group's presentation should give the board of directors a logical evaluation of the event's importance in world history.

(continued)

Differentiated Instruction for Social Studies

Welcome to the World History Hall of Fame *(continued)*

To accomplish your task, these steps must be followed:

1. First, you will be assigned to a research team.

2. Each team member will assume a role to aid in the investigation: historian, sociologist, economist, or political scientist.

3. Each team will spend six class sessions using web sites to research the event and two class sessions planning a seven-minute multimedia presentation. Final production will be done using out-of-class time.

4. Each group must turn in a bibliography of resources on the day of their presentation.

Each project must include the following four elements:

- seven-minute multimedia presentation

- annotated bibliography of all web sites

- 500-word typed paper that describes how the research was conducted and how the presentation was created and developed

- time line (1950–2000) of fifteen historical events associated with the nominated event

RESEARCH PARAMETERS

Each role has essential elements that must be addressed in the presentation:

Historian

- Who were the key individuals involved in the event?

- What were the principal causes of the event?

- How has this event influenced history since it occurred?

Sociologist

- What was society like before the event?

- How has society changed as a result of this event?

- What was the importance of technology in the event's development?

(continued)

Welcome to the World History Hall of Fame *(continued)*

Economist

- Who were the leading economic figures associated with the event?

- What did it cost, and how was it funded?

- What was the event's long-lasting economic impact?

Political Scientist

- Who were the key politicians of the time?

- Whate role did politics play during the event?

- What was the relationship between the event and the government or the nation's laws?

CONCLUSION

After completing this project, you should be able to make a strong case to say why the event you researched is worthy of being enshrined in the World History Hall of Fame.

Stop the Presses!

OVERVIEW

This is a good content lesson in either world history or U.S. history. It provides a vehicle for students to use their creativity in presenting the historical facts.

SOCIAL STUDIES STRANDS

I. Culture; II. Time, Continuity, and Change; III. People, Places, and Environments; IV. Individual Development and Identity; V. Individuals, Groups, and Institutions; VI. Power, Authority, and Governance; VIII. Science, Technology, and Society; IX. Global Connections

DIFFERENTIATION STRATEGIES

- This is a student-centered activity with independent research. The teacher is a guide to facilitate the students' self-reliance as learners.

- Multiple intelligences addressed: Verbal/Linguistic, Logical/Mathematical, Visual/Spatial, Intrapersonal

- This lesson provides flexible grouping. It lends itself to either individual or group work.

- Students can use their individual talents or strengths. Students are given choices as to how they present the material in this lesson.

- Time can be used flexibly in accordance with student levels and needs.

- Students are assessed in nontraditional ways.

WHAT TO DO

1. Students are to select a topic and prepare a newspaper or magazine article about that topic.

2. Students will need to think about the content, layout, and style of the type of presentation they select. The way a supermarket checkout tabloid presents a story is very different from the way stories are presented by *The New York Times* or *National Geographic*.

3. Students will need to think about any graphics or images they can include.

4. Students can imagine that the newspaper or magazine they choose existed in its current form in the historical time period they select. In other words, if *National Geographic* existed in 1519, how would they present the story of Cortes's arrival in Mexico and his confrontation with the Aztecs?

VARIATIONS

This lesson can be expanded to include an entire historical era. Students could create a *Time* or *Newsweek* magazine devoted to the Age of the French Revolution or the China of Shih Huang Ti with all the accompanying sections those magazines contain, such as sports, music and theater, technology, and so forth.

The student handout offers a list of topics in U.S. and world history, but you can construct your own list depending upon your curriculum.

Stop the Presses!

Directions: You have been appointed senior writer and reporter for one of the following publications: *Newsweek, National Geographic, The New York Times*, or a tabloid newspaper. Your challenge is to write a news report describing a specific historical event. You should use the writing style and layout of the publication you choose. Think of who your readership might be while writing your report.

It is likely that your publication did not exist for the event you are reporting. Just imagine that it did. Observe the proper journalistic practice of explaining the "who," "what," "where," "when," "how," and "why" of a newsworthy event. Do not forget the headline and any illustrations that will help get your ideas across.

POSSIBLE TOPICS

World History	American History
Mary, Queen of Scots and the murder of Lord Darnley	the Boston Tea Party
Shih Huang Ti and the Great Wall of China	the Battle of Gettysburg
the sinking of the *Titanic*	the completion of the Transcontinental Railroad
the Boer War	the Dred Scott decision
the Meiji Period in Japan	Cortes' arrival in Mexico
Louis XVI's escape during the French Revolution	Lewis and Clark reach the Pacific
Martin Luther writes the 95 Theses	the opening of Ellis Island
the sack of Rome	the stock market crash of 1929
the death of Socrates	the election of Andrew Jackson
the invention of Watt's steam engine	the Salem witch trials
the death of Charlemagne	
the founding of the nation of Israel	
Stanley meets Dr. Livingstone	

Write the event you chose here:

_____

Lesson 8

Differentiated Instruction for Social Studies

Tax Cut or Public Works Investment?

OVERVIEW

This lesson can culminate in a debate or a persuasive essay. Students are told that the U.S. Congress is torn between putting into place a $600 million tax cut or using that money to sponsor public works projects.

SOCIAL STUDIES STRANDS

I. Culture; III. People, Places, and Environments; V. Individuals, Groups, and Institutions; VI. Power, Authority, and Governance; VII. Production, Distribution, and Consumption; VIII. Science, Technology, and Society; X. Civic Ideals and Practices

DIFFERENTIATION STRATEGIES

- This is a student-centered activity. The teacher is a guide to facilitate students' self-reliance as learners.

- Multiple intelligences addressed: Verbal/Linguistic, Logical/Mathematical, Visual/Spatial, Interpersonal, Intrapersonal, Naturalist

- Students are encouraged to problem-solve, and multiple perspectives on ideas and events are acknowledged.

- Multiple-option assignments are used. Students are given a variety of ways to pursue the concepts in this lesson.

- This lesson provides flexible grouping. This project can be done in groups of any size, which can be determined by class size and student levels.

- Time can be used flexibly in accordance with student levels and needs.

- Assessment is by nontraditional means.

WHAT TO DO

Students can be assigned to groups or can work individually. Assign each group or student to support either the tax cut or the public works projects. Each group must address the following questions:

1. What are the benefits to the society as a whole of this spending plan?

Differentiated Instruction for Social Studies

2. What are the ramifications to the national budget?

3. Why is this money wisely spent on either a tax cut or a public works project?

4. If they support a tax cut, what income categories should receive this tax cut? Should it be across all income levels?

5. If they support public works, what kinds of projects should be designed?

ASSESSMENT

Students should justify their decisions with clear arguments and data. If they support public works, they should state what the project or projects are. Some examples might be a new mall or museum designed especially for people with disabilities, rebuilding the George Washington Bridge, a "Big Dig" such as that built in Boston to expand and depress a highway under a city, the design of a new World Trade Center, a Traditional Neighborhood Development (TND) to provide affordable housing, or a new national park to preserve open space and animal/plant species. If they support the tax cut, they should be able to explain trickle-down economics and provide a persuasive argument explaining the benefits of this budget plan.

Tax Cut or Public Works Investment?

Directions: The U.S. Congress is debating the new budget. They are in disagreement over whether $600 million should be earmarked for a tax cut or one or more public works projects. You must take one side or the other and support your decision with clear, supporting data.

Complete the questions below to argue your choice. Then, depending on instructions from your teacher, debate the question in class or write a persuasive essay defending your choice.

1. We choose to spend the $600 million for _____.
   (a tax cut or public works projects?)

2. How would this spending plan benefit the U.S. economy?

3. What parts of society would most benefit from such a plan, or would it be beneficial across all income levels?

4. What region or regions of the United States would gain the most from this plan?

5. If you choose a public works project, what is it, where would you place it, and why should it be built?

6. If you choose a tax cut, give concrete examples to explain how this would benefit the United States as a whole and be a wise decision on the part of the government.

Differentiated Instruction for Social Studies

The Powers of Congress

OVERVIEW

This lesson is designed to introduce students to the constitutional powers of the government, specifically the powers of Congress. It helps them relate the Constitution as a document to its ramifications in real life. It is a document that has had—and will continue to have—an impact on the everyday life of all citizens and residents of the United States.

SOCIAL STUDIES STRANDS

V. Individuals, Groups, and Institutions; VI. Power, Authority, and Governance; X. Civic Ideals and Practices

DIFFERENTIATION STRATEGIES

- This is a student-centered activity. The teacher is a guide to facilitate students' self-reliance as learners.

- This lesson provides flexibility in grouping. It can be done in groups or individually.

- Multiple intelligences addressed: Verbal/Linguistic, Musical/Rhythmic, Interpersonal, Intrapersonal

- Students are encouraged to problem-solve, and multiple perspectives on ideas and events are encouraged.

- Multiple-option assignments are used. Students have a choice of ways to pursue this topic and present their findings.

- Assessment is by nontraditional means.

WHAT TO DO

Students are given a list of tasks to complete in class or at home. This lesson can be modified for group or individual work, but working in pairs or small groups is the best way to facilitate brainstorming and sharing of creative ideas with the rest of the class.

ASSESSMENT

You may want to assess students on their rap, song, or cheer, how well it expresses a constitutional power, or their class discussion of which powers they think are most important.

The Powers of Congress

Directions: The powers of Congress are outlined in Article I of the U.S. Constitution. At home or in class, complete the following tasks:

1. Read Article I, Section 8 of the Constitution, provided on the next page.

2. In the space below, brainstorm examples of specific actions Congress has taken that match the powers assigned in this article.

3. Determine which three powers you think are the most important ones granted to Congress by the Constitution. Write them below.

In class with your partner(s), if any:

4. Share the powers you think are most important.

5. Identify one of those powers as the most important of all.

6. Create a rap, song, poem, or cheer that explains and justifies your choice.

Be prepared to perform your rap, song, poem, or cheer in class.

Activity 11: The Powers of Congress

42

Differentiated Instruction for Social Studies

The Powers of Congress

(From Article I, Section 8 of the U.S. Constitution)

The Congress shall have Power

1. To lay and collect Taxes, Duties, Imposts and Excises, to pay the Debts and provide for the common Defence and general Welfare of the United States; but all Duties, Imposts and Excises shall be uniform throughout the United States;

2. To borrow Money on the credit of the United States;

3. To regulate Commerce with foreign Nations, and among the several States, and with the Indian Tribes;

4. To establish a uniform Rule of Naturalization, and uniform Laws on the subject of Bankruptcies throughout the United States;

5. To coin Money, regulate the Value thereof, and of foreign Coin, and fix the Standard of Weights and Measures;

6. To provide for the Punishment of counterfeiting the Securities and current Coin of the United States;

7. To establish Post Offices and post Roads;

8. To promote the Progress of Science and useful Arts, by securing for limited Times to Authors and Inventors the exclusive Right to their respective Writings and Discoveries;

9. To constitute Tribunals inferior to the supreme Court;

10. To define and punish Piracies and Felonies committed on the high Seas, and Offences against the Law of Nations;

11. To declare War, grant Letters of Marque and Reprisal, and make Rules concerning Captures on Land and Water;

12. To raise and support Armies, but no Appropriation of Money to that Use shall be for a longer Term than two Years;

13. To provide and maintain a Navy;

14. To make Rules for the Government and Regulation of the land and naval Forces;

15. To provide for calling forth the Militia to execute the Laws of the Union, suppress Insurrections and repel Invasions;

(continued)

Lesson 10
Differentiated Instruction for Social Studies

© 2006 Walch Publishing

The Powers of Congress (continued)

16. To provide for organizing, arming, and disciplining, the Militia, and for governing such Part of them as may be employed in the Service of the United States, reserving to the States respectively, the Appointment of the Officers, and the Authority of training the Militia according to the discipline prescribed by Congress;

17. To exercise exclusive Legislation in all Cases whatsoever, over such District (not exceeding ten Miles square) as may, by Cession of particular States, and the Acceptance of Congress, become the Seat of the Government of the United States, and to exercise like Authority over all Places purchased by the Consent of the Legislature of the State in which the Same shall be, for the Erection of Forts, Magazines, Arsenals, dock-Yards, and other needful Buildings;—And

18. To make all Laws which shall be necessary and proper for carrying into Execution the foregoing Powers, and all other Powers vested by this Constitution in the Government of the United States, or in any Department or Officer thereof.

Differentiated Instruction for Social Studies

Worse Than Slavery

OVERVIEW

One of the most important social studies skills is the ability to analyze a primary source document. In this lesson, students will be asked to analyze a political cartoon and identify the social problems and issues facing the United States during the process of Reconstruction after the Civil War. Students will also be asked to identify the social problems and issues facing freedmen during the process of Reconstruction.

SOCIAL STUDIES STRANDS

I. Culture; II. Time, Continuity, and Change; IV. Individual Development and Identity; V. Individuals, Groups, and Institutions; VI. Power, Authority, and Governance; X. Civic Ideals and Practices

DIFFERENTIATION STRATEGIES

- This is a student-centered activity. The teacher is a guide to facilitate students' self-reliance as learners.

- Multiple intelligences addressed: Verbal/Linguistic, Visual/Spatial, Interpersonal, Intrapersonal

- Students are encouraged to problem-solve, and multiple perspectives on ideas and events are acknowledged.

- Multiple-option assignments are used. Students are given a variety of ways to pursue the concepts in this lesson.

- Time for this lesson can be flexible in accordance with the students' levels and needs.

- This lesson provides an opportunity for students to use their skills and knowledge of the subject area to make reflective observations.

- Assessment is by nontraditional means and involves peer assessment.

WHAT TO DO

Students are provided with copies of Thomas Nast's political cartoon "Worse Than Slavery." You should also provide students with blank drawing paper and marking pens or pencils. You may wish to make an overhead copy of the cartoon on the student page to project on a screen. There are also many web sites that include this cartoon as well as other political cartoons of the times.

Lesson 11
Differentiated Instruction for Social Studies

1. You may want to open this lesson by reviewing the historical facts of this time period (Reconstruction), emphasizing the conditions of freedmen and whites in the post-Civil War South.

2. Pass out the activity sheet with the political cartoon "Worse Than Slavery." You may also project it on a screen. Have students view the cartoon and write about everything they see in this cartoon. Allow between two and five minutes for this; then ask students what they have observed.

3. Have students analyze the cartoon and answer the questions on page 48.

VARIATIONS

After you collect the students' cartoons, you may mount them on heavy paper so that they can be passed around the room. A comment sheet could be attached to each project. Eventually, students should receive their own cartoons with comments from their classmates. This could lead to further discussion about conditions in the South during Reconstruction.

ASSESSMENT

You may want to assess students on their observations regarding the cartoon, their responses to the questions, or their original cartoons.

Worse Than Slavery

This cartoon was published in a popular nineteenth-century weekly magazine called *Harper's Weekly*. The original publication date of this cartoon by Thomas Nast was October 24, 1874.

Directions: Write your observations about this cartoon below. Be sure to write everything you notice about the cartoon and what it shows.

_____

_____

_____

_____

_____

_____

_____

Worse Than Slavery

Directions: Analyze the political cartoon "Worse Than Slavery" by answering the following questions.

1. Explain the problem in the South shown by the two figures shaking hands.

2. What are some of the reasons for the way they are dressed?

3. What parts of this cartoon make the point that the problems of Southern Blacks in the years after 1865 were worse than slavery?

4. What other problems or conditions in the South might have made life for former slaves worse than when they were slaves? You may refer to any outside reading or class work in answering this.

5. Do you think that life was actually worse for freedmen in the South in the late 1800s compared with their lives as slaves?

Make Your Own Political Cartoon
Choose one of the issues you have written about on this worksheet. Draw your own political cartoon on this subject. (Don't worry about artistic skills—stick figures are fine. The important part is the message of your cartoon.)

Differentiated Instruction for Social Studies

Make Your Own Revolution

OVERVIEW

One of the most complex historical topics to teach in world or European history classes is the series of revolutions that occurred in England, France, and Russia. The events are so complicated and convoluted that students often find it hard to discern the issues behind each revolution and why it was so hard to form a new government after the elimination of the old ruling power. This lesson is designed to help students gain an empathy for the different factions vying for rights and power and to see each group's agenda.

SOCIAL STUDIES STRANDS

I. Culture; II. Time, Continuity, and Change; III. People, Places, and Environments; V. Individuals, Groups, and Institutions; VI. Power, Authority, and Governance; VII. Production, Distribution, and Consumption; X. Civic Ideals and Practices

DIFFERENTIATION STRATEGIES

- This is a student-centered activity. The teacher is a guide to facilitate students' self-reliance as learners.

- Multiple intelligences addressed: Verbal/Linguistic, Bodily/Kinesthetic, Interpersonal, Intrapersonal, Naturalist

- Students are encouraged to problem-solve, and multiple perspectives on ideas and events are acknowledged.

- This lesson provides flexible grouping. This project can be done in groups of any size, which can be determined by the class size and student levels.

- Time can be used flexibly in accordance with student levels and needs.

- This lesson provides an opportunity for students to use their skills and knowledge of the subject area to make reflective observations.

- Assessment is by nontraditional means.

WHAT TO DO

1. Assign students into groups for each revolution, and assign pairs of students a role in that particular country. This will allow for discussion of the issues and sharing of information.

2. Have students fill out the first activity from the perspective of their assigned roles. They might even wish to assume the roles in a dramatic sense to persuade their teams to their way of thinking.

3. The group as a whole should then try to determine a system of government that is amenable to all and protects the rights of all. Not an easy task!

Revolution	Possible roles for students
English Civil War of 1642	Puritan gentry Anglican aristocrat townsman Anglican bishop yeoman farmer member of Parliament
French Revolution of 1789	peasant urban artisan bourgeois lawyer aristocrat parish priest bishop
Russian Revolution of March, 1917	peasant merchant aristocratic landowner Bolshevik member of the Social Revolutionary Party member of the Constitutional Democrat Party (Cadets)

You can add other roles or other revolutions as you see fit according to your curriculum. These are suggestions only.

Differentiated Instruction for Social Studies

Make Your Own Revolution

Directions: In your study of revolution, you will be assigned a role. You might be a peasant or an aristocratic landowner or a clergyman. Answer the following questions based on your character's specific aims in the way of reform and rights. Be prepared to defend your ideas. Why should your objectives take precedence over those of other groups?

1. Your role: _____

2. Kind of government you wish: _____

   (for example—monarchy, constitutional monarchy, dictatorship, republican democracy)

3. Should there be a constitution? Why or why not?

   _____
   _____

4. Who or what will hold executive power in the new government?

   _____
   _____

5. Who or what will hold the legislative power in the new government?

   _____
   _____

6. Who or what will hold the judicial power in the new government?

   _____
   _____

7. Who will have the right to vote in the new government?

   _____
   _____

8. What are the qualifications for holding office?

   _____
   _____
   _____

(continued)

Lesson 12

Differentiated Instruction for Social Studies

Make Your Own Revolution *(continued)*

9. What human rights are to be guaranteed? _____

_____

_____

_____

10. How are these rights guaranteed? Who protects them?

_____

_____

_____

11. Is land reform important to you? Why or why not?_____

_____

12. What is the role of the church? _____

_____

_____

13. Is there to be total separation of church and state, or will there be a state-sponsored church?

_____

_____

14. Is military service compulsory? Why or why not?_____

_____

15. What are the qualifications to be an officer in the military? _____

_____

_____

16. Are there any other goals that you wish to achieve by the revolution?

_____

_____

_____

Differentiated Instruction for Social Studies

Make Your Own Revolution

Congratulations! Your revolution has been successful and has overthrown the old regime. Now your task is to design a constitution that meets the demands of all the social groups and factions in your country. Think about the form the government will take. Who gets to vote? Is there an executive power? a legislative power? a judicial power? What are the functions of each power? Are human rights spelled out in the constitution? Who will protect those rights?

Directions: Write a draft of a new constitution for your country. It should follow the format indicated below.

A constitution for the nation of _____

Preamble (optional)

_____

_____

_____

Executive power

_____

_____

_____

Legislative power

_____

_____

_____

Judicial power

_____

_____

_____

Bill of rights (optional)

_____

_____

_____

Lesson 12

Differentiated Instruction for Social Studies

Where Would You Place a Settlement?

OVERVIEW

This lesson is based upon geography and the environment necessary for human survival. It is designed to motivate students to think about what topography, natural resources, and strategic location would work best for a place where humans settle and live.

SOCIAL STUDIES STRANDS

III. People, Places, and Environments; VII. Production, Distribution, and Consumption

DIFFERENTIATION STRATEGIES

- This is a student-centered activity. The teacher is a guide to facilitate students' self-reliance as learners.

- Multiple intelligences addressed: Verbal/Linguistic, Visual/Spatial, Intrapersonal, Naturalist

- This lesson provides flexible grouping. It lends itself to either individual or group work.

- Students are encouraged to problem-solve using their background knowledge of the subject matter.

- Time can be used flexibly in accordance with student levels and needs.

- Assessment is by nontraditional means.

WHAT TO DO

1. Assign students to groups or have them work individually.

2. The map provided on the student page shows the actual geography of the area where Jamestown, England's first permanent North American colony, was located.

3. Ask students to evaluate each location in terms of its suitability for settlement.

Differentiated Instruction for Social Studies

The actual locations as found today are:

- Site A = Hampton, VA

- Site B = Yorktown, VA

- Site C = Jamestown, VA

- Site D = Williamsburg, VA

- The river to the east is the York River.

- The river to the west is the James River.

ASSESSMENT

Students can be assessed in muliple ways, such as on their analysis of the positive and negative features of each site, including access to the river and ocean for fishing and transportation, availability of farming land, and so forth.

Where Would You Place a Settlement?

Directions: The term *site* refers to strategic location. The term *situation* refers to the other environmental factors, such as freshwater, timber, and arable land. The map below shows the area around Jamestown, Virginia, where the first English colony in North America was located. Four locations are marked by the letters A, B, C, and D. Think about the site and situation of each location. Then answer the questions that follow.

1. Which was the location of the actual settlement of Jamestown? _____

2. Did the colonists select the best location given the geographical features of the area? Why or why not?

   _____

   _____

3. Which of the four locations would you have chosen for a settlement? Explain why you chose this site.

   _____

   _____

   _____

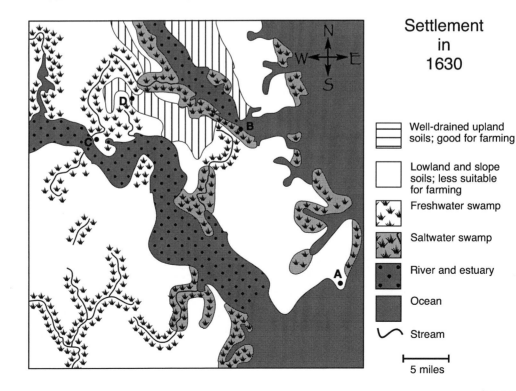

Settlement in 1630

- Well-drained upland soils; good for farming
- Lowland and slope soils; less suitable for farming
- Freshwater swamp
- Saltwater swamp
- River and estuary
- Ocean
- Stream

5 miles

Demographic Statistics on African Nations

OVERVIEW

This lesson introduces students to nations in Africa and some of the issues they face through a study of demographics. It is designed to be a data-gathering and interpretive lesson that should take between one and two class periods.

SOCIAL STUDIES STRANDS

I. Culture; II. Time, Continuity, and Change; III. People, Places, and Environments; VIII. Science, Technology, and Society

DIFFERENTIATION STRATEGIES

- This is a student-centered activity. The teacher is a guide to facilitate students' self-reliance as learners in doing independent research.

- Multiple intelligences addressed: Verbal/Linguistic, Logical/Mathematical, Visual/Spatial, Interpersonal, Intrapersonal

- Students are encouraged to problem-solve using their background skills in the subject area.

- Multiple perspectives on the data are encouraged.

- This lesson provides flexible grouping. It can be done in groups of any size or individually as determined by the class size and student levels.

- Time can be used flexibly in accordance with student levels and needs.

- Students are assessed in multiple ways.

WHAT TO DO

If you do not have computers with Internet access in your classroom, or a class set of world almanacs, you may want to reserve time in the school library or technology lab for research.

1. Start by introducing the continent of Africa to students.

2. Distribute and review the student activity pages, including the demographic terms and the data-gathering instrument. Explain the tasks that students will be performing. Be sure to clarify for your students the stages of development that countries go through.

3. Randomly assign an African country to each student or group. If using the library, introduce students to the world almanac and its various features. If using computers in the classroom or the computer lab, provide students with a list of active websites from which they can gather the data necessary for the project.

4. Once students have gathered their data, they should analyze it to determine their country's stage of development, and write a paragraph explaining how this stage fits the data they collected.

VARIATION

When all students have gathered their data, assign students to groups based on regions of Africa, such as North Africa, West Africa, and so forth. Each group should compile the results of individual countries into a table showing statistics for the whole region, then graph the results. Compare completed graphs. Is there a wide variation between regions of Africa? If so, what might account for the variation?

ASSESSMENT

You can assess students on their data-gathering, their analysis, or their paragraphs. An optional scoring rubric is included on page 59.

Scoring Rubric: Graphing Demographic Statistics

Category	4	3	2	1
Data gathering	All required data have been collected and recorded on the table.	Most required data have been collected and recorded on the table, but some gaps remain.	Some data have been collected and recorded on the table, but many gaps remain.	No data have been collected and recorded on the table.
Accuracy of data	All data are accurate and are recorded correctly.	Most data are accurate and are recorded correctly, but there are some errors.	Some data are accurate, but there are many errors.	Most data are inaccurate or incorrectly recorded.
Calculating increase or decrease	The change between the two years on the chart has been accurately calculated and has been labeled as an increase or decrease for each piece of information.	The change between the two years on the chart has been accurately calculated and labeled as an increase or decrease for some pieces of information, but not for all.	The change between the two years has been inaccurately calculated or has not been labeled as an increase or decrease for most pieces of information.	The change between the two years has not been calculated or labeled as an increase or decrease.
Analysis	Analysis addressed all questions and drew relevant conclusions from the information.	Analysis addressed most questions and drew some relevant conclusions from the information.	Analysis addressed some questions, but not all, and did not draw relevant conclusions from the information.	No analysis was done.
Development stage	The development stage chosen fits all the demographic data on the table.	The development stage chosen fits most of the demographic data on the table, but not all.	A development stage was chosen, but it does not fit most of the demographic data on the table.	No development stage was chosen.
Student-written paragraph	Paragraph clearly explains why the chosen development stage applies to the country, and addresses all elements in the description of the stage.	Paragraph explains why the chosen development stage applies to the country, and addresses most , but not all, elements in the description of the stage.	Paragraph does not clearly explain why the chosen development stage applies to the country and addresses few elements in the description of the stage.	No paragraph was written.

Demographic Statistics on African Nations

Directions: Your task is to research your assigned African country and determine its stage of development. To do so, you will need to accurately acquire statistical information, analyze it, and use it to determine the stage of development. You will need to find the following information for your country for two different years.

DEMOGRAPHIC TERMS

Literacy rate: the percentage of people who can read and write

Life expectancy: the number of years a person is expected to live

Death rate: the number of people who die each year, per 1,000 inhabitants; a high death rate is 30–35 per 1,000; a low death rate is 10 per 1,000.

Birthrate: the number of children born each year, per 1,000 inhabitants. A high birth rate is 35–50 births per 1,000; a low birth rate is 10 births per 1,000.

Net migration change: the difference between the number of people who enter and leave a country during the year, per 1,000 inhabitants; a high migration rate, either positive (more people enter the country than leave) or negative (more people leave the country than enter) can affect the overall level of population change.

Population growth rate: the change in population from one year to the next; it is usually based on birth rate, minus death rate, plus net migration rate.

Infant mortality rate: the number of children per 1,000 births who die before the age of one year; a high infant mortality rate is 100–150 per 1,000 births; a low infant mortality rate is 2–8 per 1,000 births.

STAGES OF DEVELOPMENT

Stage I: Stage I countries are generally characterized by high birth rates, high death rates, high infant mortality rates, short life expectancies for both men and women, and low literacy rates.

Stage II: Stage II countries are generally characterized by having high birth rates, declining death rates, declining infant mortality rates, lengthening life expectancies for both men and women, and rising literacy rates.

(continued)

Demographic Statistics on African Nations *(continued)*

Stage III: Stage III countries are generally characterized by declining birth rates, declining death rates, declining infant mortality rates, lengthening life expectancies for both men and women, and rising literacy rates.

Stage IV: Stage IV countries are generally characterized by low birth rates, low death rates, low infant mortality rates, long life expectancies for both men and women, and high literacy rates.

	Year 1	Year 2	Change (Increase/Decrease)
Country name: _____			
Birth rate (per 1,000 inhabitants)			
Death rate (per 1,000 inhabitants)			
Net migration rate (per 1,000 inhabitants)			
Population growth rate (birth rate − death rate + net migration rate)			
Infant mortality rate (per 1,000 births)			
Literacy rate			
Male life expectancy			
Female life expectancy			
Overall life expectancy			

Once you have gathered all the statistics, analyze them to see what they tell you about the country. To do this, answer the following questions.

(continued)

Demographic Statistics on African Nations *(continued)*

QUESTIONS TO CONSIDER

1. How did the country's birth and death rate change?

   _____

   _____

2. Beyond natural causes of death, what factors might cause a high death rate?

   _____

   _____

3. What does a negative net migration rate tell you about a country?

   _____

   _____

4. What does a positive net migration rate tell you about a country?

   _____

   _____

5. What does a negative population growth rate tell you about a country's population?

   _____

   _____

6. What does a positive population growth rate tell you about a country's population?

   _____

   _____

7. How did the country's literacy rate change? What might account for a change in a country's literacy rate?

   _____

   _____

As countries develop, they usually go through several stages. Use your data and analysis to determine your country's stage of development. (If your information does not neatly fit one of the stages described on the preceding page, choose the stage you think is closest.) Then write a paragraph explaining your country's stage of development. Be sure to address all the elements in the description of that stage.

Differentiated Instruction for Social Studies

Points of Longitude and Latitude

OVERVIEW

This lesson is skills-based and teaches the concept of absolute location as well as latitude and longitude. It is designed to take one class period, but time allotted can be flexible.

SOCIAL STUDIES STRAND

III. People, Places, and Environments

DIFFERENTIATION STRATEGIES

- This is a student-centered activity. The teacher is a guide to facilitate students' self-reliance as learners.
- Multiple intelligences addressed: Logical/Mathematical, Visual/Spatial
- This lesson provides flexible grouping. It can be done either individually or in groups.
- Time for completion of this project can be flexible in accordance with student levels and needs.
- A variety of instructional materials is used.
- Assessment is by nontraditional means.

What To Do

1. It is recommended that you have the following materials to implement this lesson: a class set of the "Points of Longitude and Latitude" student activity sheet, 1/4" graph paper and an overhead slide of graph paper, an overhead projector, marking pens, and a screen or white board.

2. Distribute the activity sheet. Begin by going over the concept of absolute location with students. Absolute location refers to employing the geographic grid system to accurately locate places on a map. It is a precise measurement.

3. Distribute graph paper and display an overhead slide of graph paper (optional). Guide students through the process of setting up the grid system on the graph paper. You could have students complete their drawing for homework.

Lesson 15

Differentiated Instruction for Social Studies

© 2006 Walch Publishing

Points of Longitude and Latitude

Directions: Your task is to plot the following points of longitude and latitude on the graph paper, then connect them using a straightedge. When plotted correctly, you will have drawn a map of one of Earth's continents.

SETUP

1. Hold your sheet of graph paper so that the short edge ($8\frac{1}{2}$ inches) is at the top and the long edge (11 inches) is on the sides.

2. Starting at the top left side of the paper, number each vertical line of the graph paper using units of two. That is, each line is worth two units. Begin with the number 90, then 88, then 86, and so forth, ending with the number 30.

3. Starting at the top right side of the paper, number each horizontal line of the graph paper using units of two. Again, each line is worth two units. Begin with the number 14, and number each line by twos until you reach 0. Then, begin numbering from 0 to 66 by twos. The numbers above the 0 will be North. The numbers below will be South.

4. Once you have done that, plot the following coordinates:

1. 12° N, 70° W	11. 9° S, 34° W	21. 35° S, 55° W	31. 53° S, 68° W
2. 10° N, 61° W	12. 10° S, 35° W	22. 35° S, 58° W	32. 55° S, 66° W
3. 8° N, 60° W	13. 13° S, 38° W	23. 36° S, 56° W	33. 56° S, 70° W
4. 6° N, 54° W	14. 20° S, 40° W	24. 38° S, 58° W	34. 50° S, 75° W
5. 4° N, 52° W	15. 23° S, 43° W	25. 39° S, 62° W	35. 20° S, 70° W
6. 0°, 50° W	16. 23.5° S, 46° W	26. 41° S, 62° W	36. 10° S, 78° W
7. 1° S, 46° W	17. 25° S, 48° W	27. 41° S, 65° W	37. 6° S, 82° W
8. 3° S, 40° W	18. 26° S, 48° W	28. 45° S, 65° W	38. 0°, 80° W
9. 5° S, 37° W	19. 30° S, 50° W	29. 46° S, 67° W	39. 10° N, 75° W
10. 5° S, 34° W	20. 32° S, 52° W	30. 47° S, 65° W	40. 12° N, 72° W

5. Now, connect the points in numerical order. What continent have you drawn? _____

6. To complete your map, add the following places:

Tropic of Capricorn: 23.5° S	the equator: 0° degrees
Buenos Aires: 34° S, 58° W	Santiago: 33° S, 71° W
Mount Aconcagua: 32° S, 70° W	São Paulo: 24° S, 47° W
Montevideo: 35° S, 56° W	Quito: 0°, 78° W
Rio de Janeiro: 22° S, 43° W	Bogota: 4° N, 74° W

Differentiated Instruction for Social Studies

Creating Climographs

OVERVIEW

This is a skills-based lesson that investigates the concept of climate. It can be accomplished in one class period or assigned for homework.

SOCIAL STUDIES STRANDS

III. People, Places, and Environments; IX. Global Connections

DIFFERENTIATION STRATEGIES

- Multiple intelligences addressed: Verbal/Linguistic, Logical/Mathematical, Visual/Spatial, Naturalist

- Students are encouraged to problem-solve independently.

- Students are encouraged to use essential skills in this subject area to understand key concepts and principles.

- This lesson provides flexible grouping. It can be done in groups or individually, which can be determined by class size and student levels.

- Time can be used flexibly in accordance with student levels and needs.

- Students are assessed in multiple ways.

WHAT TO DO

1. Review the concepts of "weather" and "climate." Present definitions of weather, climate, temperature, and precipitation.

2. Describe the tasks students will be performing. If you wish, display the completed climograph of Boston, Massachusetts as a model for students. Be sure to highlight the required components of the graph: appropriate scales on *y*-axes, proper labeling of all axes, a title.

3. If necessary, model the steps required to create a climograph, including both a bar graph and a line graph.

4. Distribute and review climatic data, and assign a city to each student. If students do not have access to a graphing program on the computer, distribute graph paper. Have students begin graphing the data.

5. Have students share their completed graphs. Then ask students to answer the questions about interpreting climatic data.

© 2006 Walch Publishing

Annual Average Temperature and Precipitation Statistics for Selected World Cities

	Jan	Feb	Mar	Apr	May	Jun	Jul	Aug	Sep	Oct	Nov	Dec
Bangkok, Thailand												
Temperature (°F)	78.8	81.7	84.6	86.2	85.3	84.2	83.5	83.3	82.6	81.9	80.4	77.9
Precipitation (inches)	0.4	1.1	1.2	2.8	7.5	6.0	6.2	7.4	12.6	9.1	2.3	0.4
Moscow, Russia												
Temperature (°F)	13.5	15.6	24.6	39.9	54.0	61.3	65.3	62.1	51.6	39.6	28.4	18.5
Precipitation (inches)	1.4	1.1	1.3	1.5	2.0	2.6	3.2	2.8	2.3	2.0	1.7	1.7
Cairo, Egypt												
Temperature (°F)	56.8	59.4	63.3	70.5	76.5	81.1	82.2	82.2	79.3	74.7	66.4	59.2
Precipitation (inches)	0.2	0.1	0.1	0.1	0.0	0.0	0.0	0.0	0.0	0.0	0.1	0.2
Baghdad, Iraq												
Temperature (°F)	48.9	53.2	61.2	70.9	81.9	90.1	94.3	93.6	87.4	76.8	63.0	52.0
Precipitation (inches)	1.1	1.1	1.1	0.7	0.3	0.0	0.0	0.0	0.0	0.1	0.8	1.0
Washington, D.C.												
Temperature (°F)	30.7	33.4	43.2	52.7	62.1	70.9	75.6	74.1	66.9	54.9	45.3	35.4
Precipitation (inches)	2.7	2.7	3.1	3.1	4.0	3.9	3.5	4.0	3.4	3.3	3.2	3.1

Differentiated Instruction for Social Studies

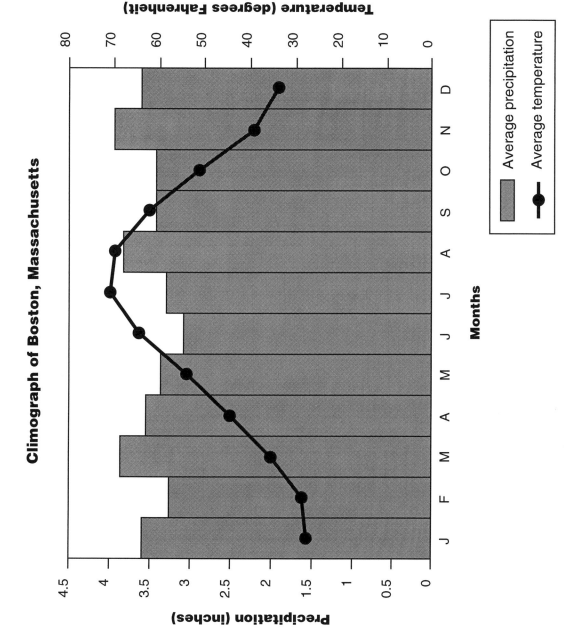

Climograph of Boston, Massachusetts

Temperature (degrees Fahrenheit)

Precipitation (inches)

Months

☐ Average precipitation
●— Average temperature

Creating Climographs

INTERPRETING CLIMATIC DATA

Directions: Using climate data provided by your teacher, create a climograph for the city you have been assigned. After drawing your climograph, use the data to respond to the following statements and/or questions. Be sure to give complete answers.

1. Review the temperature and precipitation data. Then write one or two sentences to describe the type of climate you would expect to find in each city.

   Bangkok, Thailand:

   Moscow, Russia:

   Cairo, Egypt:

   Baghdad, Iraq:

   Washington, D.C.:

2. Choose one of the five cities and plan a trip to that city. How would you need to prepare for your visit in terms of clothing needed, historical places to visit, and so forth?

3. How does the climate found at each location affect the inhabitants' living conditions? Pay particular attention to changes in seasons.

4. What conclusions can you draw about the relationship between precipitation and temperature?

Differentiated Instruction for Social Studies

A Lesson in Archaeology: Build Your Baulk

OVERVIEW

On an archaeological dig, one wall of each excavation site is left as an intact record of the strata (levels of civilization) that have been removed. This is called a baulk. Tags are placed on the wall, indicating the places where major objects were discovered at each level. In this exercise, we use the baulk to indicate the evolution of human culture in the Middle East. This exercise shows students how archaeologists work and what cultural artifacts could be found from the earliest societies in history.

SOCIAL STUDIES STRANDS

I. Culture; II. Time, Continuity, and Change; III. People, Places, and Environments; VII. Production, Distribution, and Consumption; VIII. Science, Technology, and Society

DIFFERENTIATION STRATEGIES

- This is a student-centered activity. The teacher is a guide to facilitate students' self-reliance as learners.

- Multiple intelligences addressed: Verbal/Linguistic, Visual/Spatial, Bodily/Kinesthetic, Interpersonal, Intrapersonal, Naturalist

- Multiple-option assignments are used. There is a variety of ways to approach this lesson and for the student to present his or her conclusions.

- This lesson provides flexible grouping. It can be done in groups or individually.

- Students are encouraged to problem-solve, and multiple perspectives on ideas are encouraged.

- Time can be used flexibly in accordance with student levels and needs.

- Assessment is by nontraditional means.

WHAT TO DO

This lesson can be done as group work or individually. Students could also "build" this baulk on a large sheet of cardboard or make a clay model. You could add other artifacts as well, such as sun-dried brick, a clay oil lamp, or a stone statue of a god. You could also have students construct a baulk and possible artifacts that would be found at different levels in another time and place, such as nineteenth-century New York or twentieth-century China.

The answers below give the possible configuration. The idea is to stress that culture progressed from simple to complex—for example, first copper, then bronze, and then iron tools.

ANSWERS

I. glass bottle, iron weapon, horseshoe

II. bronze spear tip

III. kiln-dried brick, shard of hand-coiled pottery, pottery beads, clay sickle, pottery fertility goddess statue

IV. flint flakes, bone beads, stone mortar

A Lesson in Archaeology: Build Your Baulk

Archaeology is a destructive science. Once objects are unearthed, they can never again be returned to the site in exactly the same way. While the dig is in progress, one wall of the excavation is left as a record of the layers that have already been removed. In that way, the archaeologist can clearly see the many levels, or strata, already unearthed. The wall that is left as a record is called a *baulk.* Tags are placed on the baulk to show the locations of important artifacts that have already been removed.

Directions: Here is your opportunity to create a baulk. Cut out the artifact tags below, then place them in the correct layers on the baulk diagram. Remember— as you go deeper into the earth, the artifacts you find are older. This baulk represents a dig in Mesopotamia. The deepest level dates to 10,000 B.C.E.

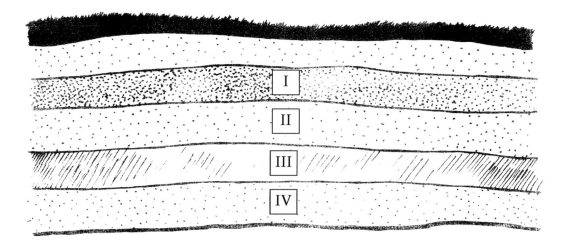

BAULK TAGS

shard of hand-coiled pottery	copper ornaments	glass bottle
tablet with writing	bronze spear tip	bone beads
clay sickle	sun-dried mud brick	horseshoe
iron weapon	kiln-dried brick	flint flakes
pottery fertility goddess statue	glazed perfume jar	pottery beads

Lesson 17

Differentiated Instruction for Social Studies

The Ellis Island Experience: A Simulation

OVERVIEW

This lesson provides students with a simulation of the trip many immigrants to the United States and the entry at Ellis Island. The year is 1907, the busiest year in the history of Ellis Island. We chose this date because it represents a peak year in immigration to the United States.

SOCIAL STUDIES STRANDS

I. Culture; II. Time, Continuity, and Change; III. People, Places, and Environments; IV. Individual Development and Identity; V. Individuals, Groups, and Institutions; VI. Power, Authority, and Governance; IX. Global Connections; X. Civic Ideals and Practices

DIFFERENTIATION STRATEGIES

- This is a student-centered activity. The teacher is a guide to facilitate students' self-reliance as learners.

- Multiple intelligences addressed: Verbal/Linguistic, Visual/Spatial, Bodily/Kinesthetic, Interpersonal, Intrapersonal

- Multiple-option assignments are used. Students are given a variety of ways to grasp the concepts in this lesson.

- Time can be used flexibly in accordance with student levels and needs.

- Students are encouraged to use their knowledge of the subject area to present reflective responses to the task at hand in this activity.

- Students' individual creativity, talents, and skills are utilized.

- Students are assessed in multiple ways.

WHAT TO DO

In this simulation, students will role-play immigrants as they prepare for a journey to the United States. They will experience the conditions of the sea voyage and go through the many checkpoints and inspections that immigrants faced at Ellis Island. Feel free to adapt this simulation to your own classroom and curriculum. We have provided an outline of the various stages of the simulation as well as reproducible sheets for the various forms and lists. The paperwork that most immigrants had to endure has been simplified to keep the paper and

72

duplication costs of this simulation at a manageable level. In some stages of the simulation, alternative activities are suggested to increase flexibility.

1. Let each student choose a role to play. We have provided a varied group of people and homelands typical of the people who might have immigrated to the United States in 1907. Included are 26 role cards, each with an immigrant's name and country, that can be cut up. Students can then draw their role card. Ask students to locate their immigrant's homeland on the world map (Activity 21) and draw a line from their country of origin to New York harbor. This preliminary exercise should give them an idea of the distance that they must travel.

2. Students should prepare for their trip by selecting what they will most need in their new land. Steamship companies usually allowed steerage passengers to take only one piece of luggage. You should set the limits—for example, one filled suitcase, cardboard box, or pillowcase. This luggage dilemma is an excellent discussion topic, for "family" groups or for the whole class. Students must set priorities and determine what the necessities for life will be in their new home (Activity 22).

3. Heads of families and single immigrants must fill out the necessary forms for entry into the United States.

4. An adult should take the role of ship captain. The captain marks the outline of a ship with masking tape on the classroom floor. Make sure the ship is small enough to become very cramped when the immigrants and their belongings come aboard. A separate, spacious first-class cabin should be outlined to demonstrate that not all immigrants came in steerage. The ship should be named and the captain given a manifest sheet (Activity 23) that lists all of the passengers. As the immigrants board, it might be interesting to have the captain tell them that because of overcrowding, they must leave one personal item behind—this often did happen. Allow students to travel in their outline ship long enough to experience the boredom and cramped conditions.

5. When it is time to disembark, it is a good idea to have adults play the roles of the various Ellis Island inspectors and authority figures, preferably adults with whom the children are not familiar—community volunteers, or teachers or administrators from another building. The presence of strangers might help students personalize the feeling of apprehension so common to arriving immigrants.

6. As they leave the ship, immigrants must be labeled with identification tags that give the name of their ship and a number corresponding to the manifest number and line upon which their name appeared. They must also be given an inspection card (both on Activity 24) that has to be stamped by immigration officials. The exception is the immigrant from England.

He should have traveled in the first-class cabin of the ship. He should not leave the cabin. The immigration inspector should come to his cabin, ask a few questions (see below), and quickly give this immigrant an inspection card admitting him to the United States. This is what happened with passengers who were wealthy enough not to travel in steerage. This may not seem fair to students, but that is the point—it is what actually happened.

7. The other immigrants must line up and go through a series of inspections. The first inspector could call out their names one at a time and compare their tags with the manifest. The medical inspection was always one of the first at Ellis Island. Public Health Service doctors checked each immigrant for signs of physical or mental illness. If a problem was suspected, the immigrant was marked with a piece of chalk—such things as the letter H for a suspected heart problem, L for lameness, X for mental defects. This could be a sensitive process for some classrooms; you may prefer to have the inspector do an overall check and scribble something on a notepad. Or, the official could draw a nonsense symbol with a piece of chalk. By not explaining the meaning of the symbol, the official can help replicate the bewilderment that immigrants felt during processing. Finally, an inspector should ask each immigrant a series of rapid-fire questions to determine the person's fitness to remain:

   1. What is your name? (The inspector should write a few names incorrectly or simplify a few. Many immigrants had their names Americanized during the inspection process whether they wished it or not.)

   2. How old are you?

   3. Where were you born?

   4. Are you married or single?

   5. What work do you do?

   6. Do you have a job waiting for you here? (A trick question, because to answer "yes" meant you were violating the Contract Labor Law of 1885. It was illegal for immigrants to take a job in the United States before they left home in order to pay for their passage.)

   7. Who paid for your passage here?

   8. Is anyone meeting you here?

   9. Where are you going?

   10. Can you read and write?

   11. Have you ever been in prison?

12. How much money do you have?

13. Show it to me.

14. Where did you get it?

15. Have you ever been deported?

If the immigrant answers these questions satisfactorily, the inspector enters the immigrant's name on the inspection card and stamps it for approval.

In reality, there were interpreters for the many immigrants who did not speak English. To simulate the language barrier, ask the inspector to express difficulty in understanding the immigrant and to repeat the question several times.

To further replicate the immigrant experience, you could detain a few immigrants for further questioning or even have some deported. Single females were not allowed to enter the United States unless someone (a relative, fiancé, or representative from an Immigrant Aid Society) was going to come for her. Immigration officials would not allow a single woman to leave alone.

Once processed, the immigrants hand in their inspection cards to a final inspector who should check it one last time and then issue landing cards. Now the immigrants are free to enter the United States legally.

VARIATIONS

Here are a few ways in which you might end this simulation:

- Have a "Welcome to America" party featuring the foods from the immigrants' native lands.

- Have the students share their feelings, either in writing or orally, about going through the Ellis Island experience.

- Have a Fourth of July party (no matter what time of year) where the immigrants can talk about what it means to be an American.

- Make a leap into the future by asking the immigrants what has happened to them since they came here. Do they wish to become U.S. citizens? Why or why not? (Remember, as many as one third of all immigrants who entered the United States emigrated back to their homelands or to another country.) A simulated naturalization ceremony could be held for those immigrants who wish to become citizens.

Here are some additional activities to do with your class:

1. Have students construct passports issued by their homeland. Every person entering this country had to have a passport from his or her country of origin. This would be a good research activity to discover each country's flag, seal, and so forth.

2. During the shipboard journey, pass around a bowl of unseasoned cooked cereal and plastic spoons. Students can try this dish to simulate the kind of food served to steerage passengers.

3. If your students know or are studying a foreign language, this might be an opportunity for them to use it. Most immigrants coming to this country did not speak English.

4. If some students do not feel comfortable role-playing the part of an immigrant, they could act as immigrant-aid officials. Many nationalities had officials in the United States who would act in immigrants' interest, helping them find housing and jobs. Representatives of these organizations could be at Ellis Island watching out for immigrants of their national background.

5. The special treatment afforded the immigrant from England could be a good topic for class discussion. Why did he receive preferential treatment? Was it his level of education? his economic status? his lack of a language barrier?

IMMIGRANT ROLE CARDS

Brigid O'Connor Single female Occupation: domestic worker Galway, Ireland	Wilhelm Ackermann Two-year-old child Erfurt, Germany	Jano Milosevic Single male Occupation: herder Visegrad, Siberia
Maria Kozlowski Mother of family of three Bydgoszcz, Poland	Domenic Masiello Single male Occupation: leather worker Salerno, Italy	Helga Ackermann Eight-year-old child Erfurt, Germany
Cecile St. Pierre Married female Guadeloupe, French West Indies	Caterina Kozlowski Twelve-year-old child Bydgoszcz, Poland	Rachel Issacshon Mother of family of two Kiev, Russia
Stenka Kozlowski Five-year-old child Bydgoszcz, Poland	Jean St. Pierre Married male Occupation: laborer Guadeloupe, French West Indies	Ara Karagosian Single male Occupation: merchant Yerevan, Armenia, Ottoman Empire
Wilhelmina Ackermann Mother of family of four Erfurt, Germany	Frederich Ackermann Father of family of four Occupation: farmer Erfurt, Germany	Michael McCrory Single male Occupation: shipyard worker Belfast, Ireland
Stefan Kozlowski Father of family of three Occupation: farmer Bydgoszcz, Poland	Johanna Ackermann Five-year-old child Erfurt, Germany	Olé Johannson Single male Occupation: farmworker Byglandsfjord, Norway
First-class passenger James Smythe-Jones Single male Recent university graduate Manchester, England	Elise Ackermann Six-year-old child Erfurt, Germany	Joshua Issacshon Twelve-year-old child Kiev, Russia
Mariush Kozlowski Ten-year-old child Bydgoszcz, Poland	Jacob Issacshon Father of family of two Occupation: tailor Kiev, Russia	Antonio Angellino Single male Occupation: laborer Naples, Italy
Spiros Zoutsoghianopoulos Single male Occupation: stonecutter Agrinion, Greece	Rebecca Issacshon Fourteen-year-old child Kiev, Russia	

The Ellis Island Experience: A Simulation

WORLD MAP

Directions: On the map, draw a line between the country your character is from and New York harbor.

The Ellis Island Experience: A Simulation

WHAT WILL YOU BRING?

Directions: Working either individually or in your "family" group, according to your role, you must decide what to bring with you to America. Most immigrants traveled in third class, or "steerage" class, and there was little space for luggage. You are allowed one piece of luggage only. What will you need? Think about what is most important to you. Families often brought a cooking pot to prepare their meals. Are there any mementos of your homeland you wish to keep? If you are a skilled worker, do you wish to bring your tools to help you get a job in your new home? List the things you wish to bring in the order of their importance in case you are asked to lighten the load and leave something out at the last minute.

Possession   **Reasons I (or my family) will need this**

_____

_____

_____

_____

_____

_____

_____

_____

_____

_____

The Ellis Island Experience: A Simulation

SHIP'S MANIFEST

Ship's Name _____

Date _____ Home Port _____

No.	Passenger	Class	Country of Origin	Occupation
01				
02				
03				
04				
05				
06				
07				
08				
09				
10				
11				
12				
13				
14				
15				
16				
17				
18				
19				
20				
21				
22				
23				
24				
25				
26				

Differentiated Instruction for Social Studies

The Ellis Island Experience: A Simulation

IDENTIFICATION TAG AND INSPECTION CARD

Ship's Name _____

Date _____

Manifest Number _____

Line Number _____

Number _____

INSPECTION CARD

(Immigrants and Steerage Passengers)

Port of Departure _____ Date of Departure _____

Name of Ship _____ Date of Arrival _____

Name of Immigrant _____

Last Residence _____

Issued and Passed at Stamp: Passed by Immigration Bureau

Port of _____ Date _____

(The following to be filled in by ship personnel prior to ship embarkation)

Ship Manifest Number _____ Line on Manifest _____

_____

The Growth of the United States

OVERVIEW

This lesson allows students a good deal of variety in how they will demonstrate that they understand a unit on the growth of the United States.

SOCIAL STUDIES STRANDS

I. Culture; II. Time, Continuity, and Change; III. People, Places, and Environments; IV. Individual Development and Identity; V. Individuals, Groups, and Institutions; VI. Power, Authority, and Governance; VII. Production, Distribution, and Consumption; VIII. Science, Technology, and Society; X. Civic Ideals and Practices

DIFFERENTIATION STRATEGIES

- This is a student-centered activity with independent research. The teacher is a guide to facilitate students' self-reliance as learners.

- Multiple intelligences addressed: Verbal/Linguistic, Logical/Mathematical, Visual/Spatial, Musical/Rhythmic, Interpersonal, Intrapersonal, Naturalist

- Students can use their individual talents or strengths. Students are given choices as to how they present the material in this multi-option assignment.

- Time can be used flexibly in accordance with student levels and needs.

- Students are assessed in a nontraditional way.

WHAT TO DO

This activity could be used as a take-home exam on this time period or as an in-class research assignment. It is designed to be done individually and not as group work to allow students to make choices best suited to their individual knowledge, skills, and talents. Simply give the activity to students to work on at home or in class.

Differentiated Instruction for Social Studies

ASSESSMENT

The following rubric is provided as an optional method of assessment.

A Portfolio Assessment on the Growth of the United States, 1865–1920

Assessment Rubric	Possible points
U.S. map	_____/25 pts
One element that looks at the expansion of business	_____/25 pts.
One element that looks at urban growth	_____/25 pts.
One element that looks at the populist movement	_____/25 pts.
One element that looks at civil and human rights	_____/25pts.
Bibliography	_____/15 pts.
Language mechanics	_____/20 pts.
Form (use of graphics, creativity, and so forth)	_____/40 pts.
Total	_____/200 pts.
Comments:	

The Growth of the United States

Directions: Choose four of the activities that follow. Make sure your choices allow you to represent as wide a breadth of knowledge as possible. Be sure to include facts and specific evidence from readings, homework assignments, class discussions, and in-class activities. Extra effort does count.

Each activity is followed by one theme, in parentheses. These are just suggestions on which theme an activity will likely represent well. You can apply any of the activity choices to any of these themes:

- expansion of business
- urban growth
- populist movement
- civil and human rights

In addition to the four choices, you must turn in a U.S. map. The map must explain U.S. territorial expansion during the 1800s. On your map, label anything you mention in your work. Be sure to label at least ten historical people, places, events, or ideas.

1. Write a feature story about a union strike during this time period. Think about the reasons for the strike and the prevailing public opinion about strikes in general. A feature story should appeal to human interest. Include anecdotes, stories, interesting facts, biographical information, and so forth. Include a picture, if possible. The minimum is 250 words. (expansion of business)

2. Draw a political cartoon looking at issues of civil and human rights. For example, compare the rights accorded to whites with those allowed to freedmen. Be sure to include specific content and context clues in your cartoon so you convey understandable information. (civil and human rights)

3. Write an editorial on the housing conditions of immigrants in major urban centers. Be sure to state a clear point of view and opinion. You can choose to write from the perspective of an immigrant, a political figure, or a reformer. The minimum is 300 words. (urban growth)

4. Use your readings to create a dialogue between a farmer and a railroad executive. This may be in the form of a rap, a poem, or a script. The minimum is 250 words. (populist movement)

5. Create a photo essay using at least seven pictures from the Web or other sources showing the change in technology as it relates to industrial

(continued)

Differentiated Instruction for Social Studies

The Growth of the United States *(continued)*

expansion. Use captions totaling less than 100 words for each photo. The caption should explain the change the invention or technological innovation had on American business. (expansion of business)

6. Write a eulogy (speech style) of a famous American. A eulogy is always quite favorable to the person who died, so use lots of adjectives to describe that person. Include references to what you "personally" remember— moments together, observations, and so forth. The minimum is 250 words. (all themes)

7. Choose two maps from this time period (1865–1920). The two maps should be related to each other, such as a resource map and a map showing industrial growth. Analyze each, and compare them in a reflection of no fewer than 300 words total. Include the maps in your portfolio. Remember, to compare does not mean to simply describe each but to show how they relate to each other. (business, populist movement, urban growth)

8. Write a letter (300 words) to your congressperson expressing how you feel about voting rights for women. Use a formal letter style, and be sure to sign your name. Of course, you must do some research to discover who represented your town in the U.S. Congress during this time period. (civil and human rights)

9. You are a commodity traveling during this time period. You might be an idea (suffrage, equal rights), a manufactured good (barbed wire, reaper), an agricultural product (wheat, corn, cotton), a resource (oil, iron ore), or anything else you know that traveled in the United States at that time. Supplement what you know with some additional research on-line, and write a day in your life. Where are you from, and where are you going? How are you being transported? Were you grown, made, or dug up? Be sure to describe how you are feeling. The minimum is 300 words. (all themes)

10. Write a song (music and lyrics) about working or living conditions in the United States during this time period. You can write about any class in society—the wealthy, the working class, the middle class, or the indigent. For those of you who are not musically gifted, you may use the music of any popular song from 1865–1920. This, of course, will require some research on your part. Your song should have three verses. (business, populist movement, urban growth)

11. Other ideas by approval of your teacher only!

What Happened Here?— A Study of Genocide

OVERVIEW

This lesson can be used as an introduction to the concept of genocide, one of the modern world's most tragic occurrences.

SOCIAL STUDIES STRANDS

I. Culture; II. Time, Continuity, and Change; III. People, Places, and Environments; IV. Individual Development and Identity; V. Individuals, Groups, and Institutions; VI. Power, Authority, and Governance; VIII. Science, Technology, and Society; IX. Global Connections; X. Civic Ideals and Practices

DIFFERENTIATION STRATEGIES

- This is a student-centered activity. The teacher is a guide to facilitate students' self-reliance as learners.

- Multiple intelligences addressed: Verbal/Linguistic, Logical/Mathematical, Visual/Spatial, Interpersonal, Intrapersonal

- This lesson provides flexibility in grouping. It can be done in groups or individually.

- Students are encouraged to problem-solve, and multiple perspectives on ideas and events are encouraged.

- Students are encouraged to use their essential skills in this subject area to provide reflective responses to the issue dealt with in this project.

- Time can be used flexibly in accordance with student levels and needs.

- Students are assessed in multiple ways.

WHAT TO DO

1. Pass out the maps provided. Then, either individually or in groups, have students try to answer the question "What happened here?" By looking at all the maps, they should be able to deduce that these are all places where genocide was committed. The maps provided show the location of the Armenian genocide (World War I); the Holocaust in Europe (World War II); the Cambodian genocide, or the "Killing Fields," of c.1979–1998;

Lesson 20

Differentiated Instruction for Social Studies

the Rwandan genocide of 1994; the attempted extermination of the Kurds by Sadam Hussein (c. 1988); and repression in Tibet under the Chinese, which has been described as cultural genocide.

2. Next, pass out the student activity sheets and go over the definition of genocide as set down in 1948. Students should fill out the activity as a springboard for a class discussion as to why the genocide took place, who were the persecuted groups, and how this event fits the United Nations definition of genocide.

3. A further step might be to look at some other event in history (for example, the push to the American West and the elimination of Native American tribes, particularly in California) and see if it constitutes genocide. You might ask students the difference between a massacre and genocide.

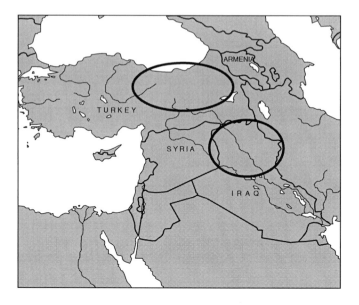

Differentiated Instruction for Social Studies

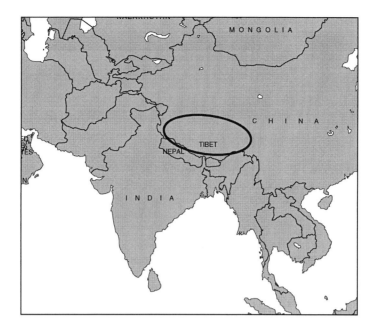

Lesson 20

Differentiated Instruction for Social Studies

What Happened Here?— A Study of Genocide

Definition of Genocide from the United Nations Convention of the Prevention and Punishment of the Crime of Genocide, 1948:

Article 2: In the present Convention, genocide means any of the following acts committed with intent to destroy, in whole or in part, a national, ethnical, racial, or religious group, as such:

   a. Killing members of the group;

   b. Causing serious bodily or mental harm to members of the group;

   c. Deliberately inflicting on the group conditions of life calculated to bring about its physical destruction in whole or in part;

   d. Imposing measures intended to prevent births within the group;

   e. Forcibly transferring children of the group to another group.

Directions: Using the definition of genocide and the maps provided, answer the following. Use additional sheets of paper, if necessary.

1. Looking at the maps, list each area a genocide took place, the persecuting powers, and the victims of the genocide. Do you know the dates?

Country or location	Power	Victims	Date

(continued)

Differentiated Instruction for Social Studies

What Happened Here?— A Study of Genocide *(continued)*

2. Take one of the genocides you listed on page 90. Tell how it fits the United Nations definition of genocide.

   _____

   _____

   _____

   _____

   _____

   _____

   _____

3. Using the same genocide as above, write a paragraph explaining why it took place. What were the motivating factors? What was the result?

   _____

   _____

   _____

   _____

   _____

   _____

   _____

4. Could any of the genocides you listed have been prevented? Who could or should have prevented it?

   _____

   _____

   _____

   _____

   _____

   _____

   _____